RAIL ROVER

SCOTLAND IN THE 1970S AND 1980S

Arnie Furniss

AMBERLEY

First published 2017

Amberley Publishing
The Hill, Stroud,
Gloucestershire, GL5 4EP

www.amberley-books.com

ISBN: 978 1 4456 6957 1 (print)
ISBN: 978 1 4456 6958 8 (ebook)

British Library Cataloguing in Publication Data.
A catalogue record for this book is available from the British Library.

Typeset in 10pt on 13pt Celeste.
Origination by Amberley Publishing.
Printed in the UK.

Contents

Introduction

Let's get this straight from the outset – this is a personal view of my own experiences and it's impossible to convey them all within this format without rivalling *War and Peace* for a word count! So this is the short version of how I got interested in trains and my favourite country, Scotland – the land that I travelled and loved in the 1970s and 1980s. Starting with excursions and special offers, ending up with rail rovers and free passes, the latter when I joined the railways, I always came back to Scotland. The Rail Rover? That would be me.

Ticket or choice of lifestyle? I leant towards the latter in the above era, when funds permitted. In reality, it was both. I don't know if any enthusiasts chose to spend their holidays actually living on trains in the days of steam, rather than just photographing them. Did rover tickets even exist then? I'm sure someone will let me know. In the 1970s, it seemed to be a realm well-suited to the diesel enthusiast willing to spend short nights on steam-heated and often crowded coaching stock. The rewards in Scotland far exceeded the discomforts.

From a few small incursions north of the border during the early 1970s, exploring a new world that seemed to my insular young mind as adventurous as the NASA space program, right up to a time in the 1990s when I could navigate the roads of the far north without a map, I felt an affinity with the country. The question is, how did I, Manchester born and bred, a 'baby boomer' child of the 1950s, end up travelling the railways of Scotland? How did I subsequently fall in love with the country, its railways and ferries? It's a long story so get a cup of something hot or a glass of something else and let's travel that journey together.

I learnt to swear before I could walk properly. An odd fact to start an account of a diesel odyssey in the aforementioned post steam period and environs, but there is a railway relevance. Until 1960, from the time of my birth in 1956, we lived above my Dad's 'Woodworker's Supplies' shop in Longsight, Manchester. The location is on the A6 and adjacent to the railway bridge that crosses it. In 1958 the bridge was replaced in a major operation involving some new – for the time – concrete technology and is now, technically, four separate bridges under each line. I digress. Next to my Dad's shop was a baker's, where the workers from the bridge construction would purchase some comestibles (pies) and stand around my pram while they ate. The two-year-old bundle of joy that was me, left outside Dad's shop in a pram to snooze my early life away (a safe thing to do in those days), copied the language of these workers, much to my Mother's horror! It would come in handy in later life. Remaining memories of the railway at that location, up to the age of four, revolve around lining up 'Matchbox cars' on the upstairs windowsill; this would be called obsessive behaviour these days. While I occupied myself in this activity, the steam trains drifted by the window in an endless procession. They were a part of everyday life. I can't honestly say they inspired me – I was more interested in my favourite toy than trains! I remember them, but they were just there, the moving wallpaper beyond the window.

In 1960, we moved from the shop to a house where I shared a bedroom with my younger brother Ron. Our room overlooked the Styal line in Levenshulme, Manchester. The trains were still just a background to growing up; steam-belching behemoths blasting past on long freight trains in the fading light as a man on a bicycle arrived in the back street to light the gas lamps. The front of the house overlooked the A34, a dual carriageway in a leafy suburb. There wasn't much traffic in those days but what traffic there was had the memorable Scammell three-wheeler tractor units that had long since replaced the railway's horses. The grass in the middle of the dual carriageway covered where the trams used to clang past, though this part of local history remained unknown to me for many years. The steam trains that passed by our bedroom window changed to diesels and electrics within the blink of an eye – the first part of the country to see the rapid evolution of railways when other areas were to be starved of this development to 'cut costs'! As a child, I was an unwitting observer to a momentous change in transport history, though in those days, I didn't have a clue about the reality of it all. Children adapt to change far quicker than adults, accepting the new as normal.

It was from this new location, at the age of four, that I met a seven-year-old Howard Heyl, who was later to have a pivotal effect on my railway enthusiasm. I watched the trains with a passive interest, while Howard seemed to have a keener view. Over the next few years we saw the engineering trains that came along, usually on a Sunday with a tank engine in charge. These trains put the stanchions in place for the wires that would be the first stage of the London Midland electrification. One enduring memory is of a steam engine parked on the bridge behind our house; the engineers were busy taking part in history while the bewhiskered, pipe smoking driver looked down on us with a benevolent smile. I could have misread this at that age, it may equally have been disdain – what did I know! Less than a quarter-mile away, we watched from Birchfield primary and junior schools as the early diesel Class 40s thundered past on their way to Euston. We thought they were called 'Mancunians' because that was the name on the headboard they carried! We didn't know what a 'Mancunian' was! It was only in my teens that as a born and bred resident of Manchester I could actually refer to myself as a Mancunian! Throughout this time, the trains were always there and, as children, we thought they were part of everyday life. Surely everyone lived the same life? We had no idea how narrow our view of the railways actually was.

My family moved to Stockport in 1968 and railways were still something that went on in the background as far I was concerned. Jubilee Sidings in Heaton Norris were close to our new house and many a night I would go to sleep listening to the cast-iron clank of the wagons as the diesel shunter rearranged them to the background sound of the chimes from the church clock – classic middle England. The sidings and the clock are long gone. It barely registered on my teenage brain!

Like the author Nicholas Whittaker, in his book *Platform Souls*, I was woken from this teenage torpor by a friend who was further down the road into the marvellous addiction that the railways provided. I was finally seduced to the atmosphere of this realm in 1972 by, you guessed it, my old mate Howard! He persuaded me to tag along with him, just for the hell of it, on an overnight journey to Bristol, Cardiff and Swindon. It changed my life forever! I had to borrow a 'fiver' off my Dad to do it. I paid him back. I always did. I can never pay Howard back for opening my eyes to an enthusiasm that I've followed on five continents up to press! He seems happy with the odd pint...

The Roving Begins...

My first venture onto Scottish rails was in March 1974, on an advertised excursion to Largs from stations in the Manchester area. We had to catch the excursion from Miles Platting which, for me, entailed staying the night at Howard's house and walking from Levenshulme to Miles Platting, which for a tender youth of eighteen, at an unearthly hour of the morning, was quite daunting! It was only about 3 miles, but it seemed longer. We were rewarded by the arrival of a pre-TOPS (Total Operational Processing System) numbered Class 40, number 308, which was to take us all the way to Largs and back in Mark 1 corridor coaching stock and I dearly wish I could remember more than my scant notes of that day provide! Mr Heyl tells me that we caught a bus to Weymss Bay and back, just for the ride! I barely remember this, though I do recall feeling how alien the town of Largs seemed at a time when my experience of the UK was somewhat limited. The differences were fascinating and somewhat hypnotic. The architecture, so different from the seaside towns of Lancashire. The food, the shops, the ferries, it was a wonderful experience. Staring in a shop window and wondering what 'soor plums' or 'clootie dumplings' were! Basically, I was out of my depth, in a complete daze, and found myself just following Howard, three years older and infinitely more worldly wise! Here, in the early days of my railway experiences in Scotland, I gave little thought to purchasing a camera.

In 1974, I was working in the operating theatre at Stockport Infirmary. My job at the time involved some mid-week days off, so when a promotional rail ticket, which encompassed a round trip to Glasgow and Edinburgh for the princely sum of £2.75, became available, it was too tempting to resist! Having said that, I'd never done such a journey on my own and my weekly wage at the time averaged £20. This was a big leap into the unknown on a solo expedition, but the fact is, I never gave it a second thought! Railway enthusiasm made me a fearless explorer, though there was a hint of peer-pressure among the fraternity, trying to outdo the latest exploit of ones contemporaries.

In the days before instant information and handheld electronic 'crutches', all I needed was a map, a timetable, a loco shed directory and the will to explore, quite happy to do it on my own if necessary. Thus equipped I made my first solo ventures to Caledonia, still without my own camera, although on a couple of occasions I did have a borrowed Instamatic that belonged to my mother! One day I'd be working in the operating theatre, dealing with road traffic accident casualties, broken bones, hip operations or kids having their tonsils removed, and the next day I'd be finding my way around the Glasgow suburbs looking for diesel depots, forgotten sheds and a few rare numbers for my Ian Allan volumes. It amazes me from this distance in time, that I was still a teenager and a few weeks away from purchasing my own camera.

Although I didn't realise it, these solo journeys had a historic note to them. It was the last gasp of diesel-hauled trains to Glasgow on the West Coast Main Line; electrification was imminent. One memorable journey involved a single Class 50 diesel on an overcrowded overnight train that made a hell of a racket going up the steep gradient to Shap Summit. Despite the wonderful noise, I was fed up with standing in the corridor for the 141 miles from Crewe. While leaning out of the window at Carlisle and feeling very jaded, I heard a station announcement regarding a relief train some 20 minutes behind us. I got off and took my chances to find myself on an empty train with another Class 50 for the rest of the trip to Glasgow and a welcome bit of shuteye! 50012 and 50021 were the locos in question for those of you that like the details!

On that particular day there was a 'bread strike' in England and a 'bus strike' in Falkirk. The casual reader may think these are unrelated events; I doubt they'll ever be seen in the same sentence again! So it was that I found myself in Falkirk without a bus journey as promised in my *Loco Shed Directory*. Having travelled this far and thinking I may never be here again (how wrong I was!), I decided to walk to Grangemouth for train spotting purposes, not realising that the effort in the poor weather would only produce a couple of 'rare' diesel shunters! Walking back through Falkirk town centre and the 'dreich' or drizzly weather, I stopped off to buy five loaves for my Mother to put in her freezer back in England. I eventually broke the dismal slog of the walk and had a pint at the 'Woodside', near Falkirk High, with some off-duty station staff, who found my drenched personae hilarious! The heat on the train to Edinburgh provided by 5394 and 27114 helped me to dry out a little. I still didn't own a camera, but I was considering obtaining one!

A few weeks later, on the first day of the summer timetable, I returned to Glasgow on 1S45, the morning service from Manchester Victoria and Liverpool Lime Street that combined into one train at Preston. An unremarkable event you may think, but 6 May 1974 wasn't just the start of the new timetable, it was the first day of electric loco hauled services to Glasgow and I was on the first electric-hauled train to arrive there! We were duly met by a welcoming committee, handing out 'Electric Scot' badges, accompanied by a solitary piper! The bagpipes are not a sound that many Southerners can listen to; you either love or hate them. I've experienced the sound in many strange locations, including the cattle hold of a ship! I am always moved by them. It says a lot about the North/South divide that the second electrically hauled train to arrive in Glasgow, which happened to originate in London, was met by a full band of pipers. I found out about this on my way home in a conversation with a fellow traveller. Ironically, the historic run on 1S45 that morning was behind 87005, later to be named *City of London*! Within minutes of my arrival in Glasgow that morning, I was already on my way to the local depots. By the time the train from London turned up, I was long gone and a mere few days away from purchasing my first camera, oddly enough, in London!

On 11 June 1974, I made another solo trip, this time to London where, after visiting some locations 'south of the river' in pursuit of train numbers – quantity against quality – I eventually found myself in a camera shop near Trafalgar Square in the days when foreign tourists were relatively scarce and a customer was just that, a 'customer'. I must have been one of their youngest punters at the age of eighteen, but they were very forgiving and helpful. I'd already looked at camera prices in Manchester and, to my surprise, they were similar in central London! I purchased a Yashica GTN rangefinder camera, identical to Howard's, and two black and white Ilford FP4 films. Suitably equipped and with some slide film in my mother's Instamatic for back up, I descended on Old Oak Common to start my first, tentative steps along a photographic road that I'm still travelling. I'm still making mistakes, too! Back home, Howard guided me through the process of developing the film and printing my first efforts.

The badge handed out to passengers arriving at Glasgow on the first day of electric Inter-City services.

Into Battle! Intensive Roving!

With my new technology, a dubious collection of film, an unwieldy tripod and a big bag, I set off in August 1974 on the first venture to the far north of Scotland on an all-line rover as part of a four man team! That should probably read 'one man and three teenagers' – Mr Heyl, at twenty-one, was the elder statesman of the group and in charge of the timetable. It was my first holiday that didn't involve the family. I had a new family now, though I was too young to realise it. Apart from a day excursion to Southend in 1975, I've not seen two members of the 1974 contingent to the present day! I met many more folk in Scotland over the years and see some of them occasionally at diesel events on preserved railways. We meet as though mere minutes have passed since the 1970s.

The people in this ever-growing world of rail rovers, be they enthusiasts or railwaymen, formed a loose bond at first, building up over the years, to create, for want of a better term, a brotherhood – a grossly inadequate expression for the camaraderie that survives to the present day. It has to be said that there was an occasional woman that shared our interest, including my first wife, but they were few and far between.

Roving the rails of the entire UK as an eighteen-year-old was an incredible learning experience and Scotland had a particular, unique attraction. August 1974 was very overcast compared to the following two years, though I was so preoccupied that I didn't notice until forty years later looking back at my efforts. Nevertheless, the trips within Scotland, including sailing on Loch Lomond and the Clyde, had a profound effect on me. Subsequent holidays up north were narrowed down to one week, sometimes two separate weeks a year when we availed ourselves of the 'Freedom of Scotland' ticket. Note that it wasn't called a 'Scottish Rover', it was a 'Freedom of Scotland' ticket, an important distinction and I doff my imaginary cap to the person or persons that came up with that title! Let's face it, this ticket wasn't meant for the likes of me, a callow youth, a member of the lumpen proletariat in the mid-1970s with a burgeoning interest in photography and trains, it was meant to attract the tourists, preferably foreign, with lots of spare cash to spend! To some extent it was also aimed at the home market for those that didn't own a car or wanted a holiday that didn't involve driving a great distance, to see the world from a train window and help the local bed and breakfast trade. There were a few that took their cars with them on the Motorail services, but they weren't 'rail rovers'. The rover tickets were not intended for we

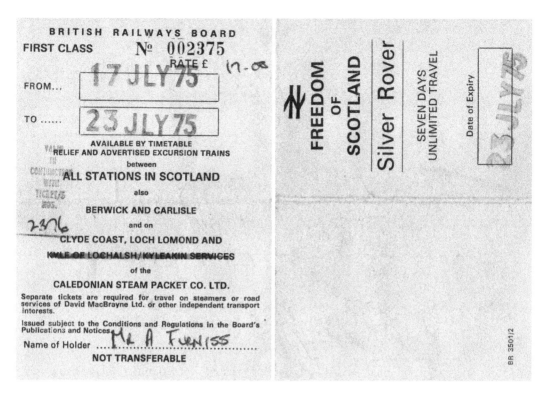

The Holy Grail of Scottish roving! £17 wouldn't get you a night out these days. In 1975, it represented half a week's wages to me! It was worth it. The overnight trains promised a better snooze in first class!

few 'diesel bashers' that were happy to snooze in a Mark 1 compartment for the night, or a small portion of the night. Either way, I suspect that the majority of rover ticket sales in the UK toward the end of the 1970s were being sold to the growing number of diesel followers. Proof of that came in the early 1980s with the creation of two to three day rover tickets covering specific areas of the UK and of little use to the tourists of the day that were abandoning the railway en masse for the comfort of their cars. Back in Scotland, and firmly on the rails, we sought some exotic traction. To those of us that lived south of Carlisle, everything north of Glasgow and Edinburgh was exotic!

We that resided in the North West of England in the late 1970s resented the loss of what were considered to be 'our' Class 50s to replace the much-loved Class 52s on the Western Region. Truth be told, after the electrification to Glasgow was complete, it was an inevitable decision, despite rumours that they might go to the Eastern Region. The rebels among us refused to follow the 50s to their new territory, despite some loyalty to the 'English Electric' brand, turning our attention to Scotland and the locomotives built by the Birmingham Railway Carriage and Wagon Company, with a few Class 40s thrown in for good measure!

The BRCW did quite well out of the general confusion of the early days of dieselisation. Their Sulzer power units shared much technology with the BR-built Type 2s and benefited from the interchangeability of spare parts and were generally reliable, though I know some older train crews might disagree with that assessment! The Class 26s seemed to plod on against anything they threw at them on the passenger trains; only 26001 to 26007 were asked to go above and beyond their design parameters on some very heavy freight trains. I only experienced one failure of a Class 26 and, on another occasion, one 27 in all the thousands of miles that I travelled behind them. The Scottish Region got their money's worth out of these plucky machines.

Eventually, some of the Class 27s were, however, severely hammered by the push/pull services between Glasgow and Edinburgh, the first services to have a diesel loco at either end of the train at a consistent high speed. The demands of the timetable took its toll on these machines which weren't really designed for such an intensive use. Fires in the engine compartment became a common problem. The Scottish Region finally decided to replace the rapidly deteriorating Class 27s with a single Class 47 on these services, incorporating a driving trailer vehicle to make the turn back at each end of the line a rapid undertaking. All went well enough until a driving trailer hit a cow at Polmont in July 1984, derailing the train and causing thirteen deaths and sixty-one injuries. Much debate was to follow about the use of driving trailers (converted coaching stock) and safety at high speed with a lightweight vehicle at the front but it came to nothing and we still have this arrangement in many places to the present day. Writing as an ex-driver, I'd rather hit some livestock at the helm of a 120 tonnes plus locomotive than a 35-ton driving trailer! Simple physics, but not to the 'number crunchers' of the modern railway who, I suspect, use the 'cost-benefit' analysis system that originated in the USA. These days they rely on fences.

A reunion. 26038 was the first Class 26 I had for haulage back in August 1974 and here it is, battling on because of the efforts of many people. Seen at Bury, on the East Lancashire Railway, in 2015! Now named *Tom Clift 1954–2012* in honour of lifelong railwayman Tom Clift, who had been appointed the new head of Hull Trains shortly before his unfortunate death. The locomotive had been one of his favourites in preservation and his family raised the money to buy and maintain the locomotive in his honour. A testament to the man.

The Politics of Diesels

The demise of steam traction in the UK and the diesel and electric evolution has been dealt with in great detail over the years and in many publications, so I'll just try to summarise it for the purposes of this volume. The nationalisation of the railways in 1948 was basically a 'paper tiger'. It had to be done but all the people from the 'Big Four' companies (London North Eastern, London Midland and Scottish, Great Western and Southern) were still in place, still had influence, and still had a remarkable amount of independence. This carried on into the 1950s' dieselisation programmes, resulting in a myriad of diesel types and a system that meant that the regions used their independent character at the expense of common sense, though it was to the advantage of diesel enthusiasts. It would take some years after a controversial chap by the name of Beeching left his scars on the country before the different regions and their independent ways would finally knuckle down and try to work together, with mixed results.

It wasn't until Richard Marsh was appointed as chairman of British Railways that the standard for the future really took hold. It was the advent of the High Speed Train that made the tide turn, only for his efforts to be ultimately thwarted. The re-branding exercises in the 1960s were nothing by comparison with the futuristic advent of the HSTs. Love them or loathe them, his HSTs live on, seen from Penzance to Inverness and Aberdeen to the present day – a testament to the man and his team.

Scotland's railways were always going to be independent, no matter who was in government, or in charge of British Railways, though they suffered as much as the other regions at the hand of Beeching when it came to line closures. By the mid-1970s, Scotland had pared down its railways and its diesels until only the Class 26s and 27s were Scotland's own, bar a few obscure diesel shunters and the Haymarket Deltics. The 26s and 27s made the odd foray south of the border, but they would always be associated with Scotland. Some earlier diesel classes could still be seen for a while, languishing in scrap lines around Glasgow. A lucky few 'Claytons' would live on as industrial shunters or find use among the bizarre collection that Derby Research Department employed. One Clayton lives on in preservation – D8568, the sole member of the class to survive, thanks to the efforts of the Diesel Traction Group. In retrospect, it seems obvious that someone at Derby Research Department had a personal interest in saving some rare traction from the cutter's torch before the diesel and electric preservationists gathered momentum. Well done, that man, or men, for I doubt there was a woman involved – such were the railways in those days! That's not a sexist comment, it's a fact relative to the railway era in the 1970s. Diesel preservation has its share of women in these enlightened days but they were few and far between in the 1970s!

I never got to see the Claytons working in Scotland, though I saw many on scrap lines around Glasgow. Thanks to the Diesel Traction Group, this one surviving member gives us a reminder of what they looked and sounded like! D8568 leaving Hampton Loade on the Severn Valley Railway, 2 October 2015.

Why are we here?
The Eternal Question!

In my case, I was here to chase diesels! By the late 1970s and early 1980s, Scotland had become a magnet for the diesel enthusiast. The Westerns were gone and the much-beloved Deltics were being displaced from the East Coast Main Line and were often found on Edinburgh to Aberdeen services, going the same way as their steam predecessors. The dwindling fleet of Class 40s were pressed into passenger service on the Aberdeen and Inverness lines that meant some spirited driving to cope with timings designed for a Class 47 or a pair of 26s! The remaining examples of Class 40s with working steam heating boilers were often 'purloined' from other regions to keep the Scottish passengers (and us!) warm. There was a great feeling of 'make do and mend' as the other regions were benefiting from electrification and cascaded motive power. These distinctions at the time were unknown to the average diesel chaser, including me! We just thought Scotland was the place to be.

The 'Freedom of Scotland' wasn't just a ticket for many of us, it was our home for at least a week! Though a handful of folk went for the comfortable attraction of a bed and breakfast in a guest house, diehards like myself and many others grabbed a few hours' sleep on one of several overnight train options. I spoke with my old friend Howard recently and mentioned this difference between the two groups of enthusiasts. He said, 'Why would you spend a night in a B&B when the trains are still running?' He has a point. It was a much nicer snooze when we splashed out £17.50 for the week on a First Class 'Silver Rover' in 1975, availing ourselves of the wonderful, though a little bit dusty (and otherwise empty) first class compartments. A few guards didn't think we were 'first class material', subjecting us to more ticket checks than the rest of the travelling public! The favourite trains were the Glasgow or Edinburgh to Inverness or vice versa – no chance of oversleeping, unlike the southbound overnights to Carlisle, which could and did end up with an unfortunate arrival at Preston or Crewe! East Coast options on a rover ticket were only valid to Berwick-on-Tweed, which was too short a distance for a viable snooze until after October 1977, when I joined the railways and could stretch a rover ticket with the help of a free pass and effect a turnback at Newcastle!

The author Tiresias, aka Roger Green, said in his excellent book about commuting to London from Oxford, 'Man is born free and is everywhere in trains'. I think he'd like the

Another first class rover; slightly more expensive and a new BR corporate image!

distinction of the Scottish ticket regarding 'freedom'! He was trapped in a long cycle of repetition yet retained his sanity by honing his observational skills and writing a book about it! I found that in many parts of Scotland – as a regular traveller, if not a commuter – one's observational skills were sapped from the system by a scenic vampire; hypnotised by the world beyond the window to the point where you're staring out of it until your cup of tea has gone cold or you're shaken from the reverie and mesmerism by a boisterous fellow traveller, the intrusion of the guard to check your ticket, or even better, by the roar of the diesel traction struggling against a gradient. This phenomenon was more prevalent north and west of Inverness. The West Highland lines held a very different spell.

Maybe it's just me. I've travelled the rails of Scotland with many people that liked to occupy their time accumulating mileage behind the locos while reading books, newspapers, or even knitting! Unless it was dark, I couldn't do that. I wanted, nay, needed, to view the passing world and tried to learn more about it as went past my window.

From 1974, Scotland, its railways and its islands, have played a very special part in my own history. I've stood on all the continents, except Antarctica, and it's always Scotland that calls me back. That first memorable journey to Thurso was very overcast, drab and drizzly but was magical nonetheless. The word 'dreich' was not yet in my vocabulary, but it certainly is now! I watched the county of Caithness roll into the distance over the 'flow country', not realising its geological significance until many years later. I sipped at the

'Slumming it' in second class, but as I've joined the railways by this time, my week's holiday (and overnight accommodation on the coaching stock!) costs the princely sum of £11.

awful cups of 'Maxpax' tea from the buffet car, washed my hands on the little slabs of green Palmolive soap in the toilets, dropped my bag on a seat, noticing the ensuing small cloud of rising dust and caught the whiffs of steam from the heating system that made the train smell of damp wood, despite the fact that it was August! It was a major turning point in my life. Never again would the comforts of home, the three channels (!) on the television or even my parents, hold any sway over my life (in my dreams!). Here, in the far reaches of the railway system, I was finding my independence. Even the poor weather was part of the experience. We soon learnt that the weather was incidental; it didn't mean less pleasure travelling, merely fewer photographs. 'I travel not to go anywhere, but to go. I travel for travels sake. The great affair is to move.' – Robert Louis Stevenson. He was referring to Scotland, of that I have no doubt.

Though I'd previously been drawn to the Strathclyde area, that first journey to Thurso on a grim day in 1974 caused me to fall in love with Scotland, travel in general, and the far north in particular! There were some other diversions in my life in the overall scheme of things at this time; the occasional love interest for example, only one of which, my first wife, shared the desire to live on trains, sometimes for weeks on end! To this day she's still an avid Deltic enthusiast! The only diversion of any note that really stopped me in my tracks was playing the bass guitar and that really is another story, pardon the puns!

People. I've met one or two all over the planet! Outside of Liverpool and Ireland, I think Scotland has a great concentration of nature's comedians and incredible hospitality. I've been really privileged to have met many of them on these railway rambles! For that reason alone I'm going to include photographs from an adventure over three memorable days with a certain Jimmy Morgan on his last few days as an Eastfield guard. The text on the photographs will provide the details...

It still has the primary title of 'Freedom of Scotland' and it's still a bargain; despite the BR privilege rate of £12, which translates to £48 for the general public, it's an undeniable bargain! You could spend the week cruising on the Clyde with this ticket and save a fortune!

The Railway Lines of Scotland

It's in my nature to go against the grain, so let's start at the top!

Thurso and Wick – two short lines after a long journey to Georgemas Junction. A few scant miles of fairly featureless farmland after the magnificence of the rest of Caithness. Doesn't sound too exciting does it? To me the very names hold a fascination. They derive from a time when the Norsemen ruled this part of the country and not that long ago in the scheme of things – less than 600 years! Though Thurso is the furthest north station in the UK, Wick is the furthest from London and, since the opening of the Channel Tunnel, there's a continuous rail link that takes the steel of the rail from Wick to Vladivostok! Outstanding! Well, it is to my small and failing brain! I'd like to do that run with a Class 52 'Western' if the track gauges permitted it. We can all dream: 'Those who dream by day are cognizant of many things which escape those who dream only by night.' – Edgar Allan Poe.

Thurso. A place I came to know intimately over the years. Be it from that first day in 1974 – which involved a quick dash around town and a quick drink in the nearest hostelry before the return journey to Inverness, or returning there on a minibus full of band personnel, guitars and equipment in 2001, to bend the ears of the good people of Orkney – Thurso holds a special place in my heart. One memorable evening in the railway days comes to mind, playing Scrabble in a bar where the Canadian barkeep refused to serve a group of Spanish trawlermen. Local politics. Deep sea fishermen that could fish stuff from our waters that we weren't allowed to catch. They were a long way from home, looking for some relaxation, finding themselves social pariahs! Serve them and lose your regular customers – not much of a choice. Heavy stuff! I lost the Scrabble game...

Wick. A road less explored. Purple sandpipers in the harbour. Fond memories of trawling the shops, mainly for food, the bridge over the river and a quick pint before the train. I bought my first guide to British birds in Wick! When the days of decent diesel traction had gone, I returned there to land and take off from the wonderful Wick airport, where the runway is crossed by a road, controlled by traffic lights.

In my diesel chasing days it was possible to do both of the single line branches from Georgemas Junction in one day by catching a bus from Thurso to Wick. I can't remember who came up with the idea but it was a stroke of genius. We did this option on several occasions, courtesy of the Highland Omnibus Company!

Thurso. There were those that tried to ride behind as many diesels as possible in the 1970s and 1980s, but a hardy few wanted to travel to the outposts of the system. Thurso and Wick took some effort. I took this photo on my first decent camera on some awful slide film and an overcast day, but I was so pleased to have made it this far north that I had to take a photograph of the station! I thought I might never be here again. How wrong I was! It turned out to be an historic shot in so many ways. The vehicles, the Scottish blue station sign, long gone. 6 August 1974. I was eighteen years old.

26036 waits to take us back to Georgemas Junction at Thurso after the first of many trips to the far north of the UK railway system. It may have been a gloomy start, but I was hooked! A brief walk around town and the seafront gave me my first view of the Pentland Firth and the island of Hoy, which I was to explore at length in later years.

Wick – further from London than Thurso though not as far north. On the left of the loco, my lifelong friend, Mr Heyl, adjusts his cap. 26022 is ready to return to Inverness on 29 September 1980. The railway used to continue from Wick to Lybster in the south, but it only lasted from 1903 to 1944 as road transport, even in that era, tended to take a more direct route.

Georgemas Junction, 6 September 1976. While waiting for the ex-Wick train to join up with our section from Thurso, we see a rare freight movement. I've no idea which Class 26 it is, but that doesn't matter at this distance in time. The guard's van, however, interests me. I joined the railways in 1977 as a freight guard and spent many a happy, if uncomfortable, hour in these 20-ton mobile sheds!

26018 arrives at Georgemas Junction from Wick, 6 September 1976. 26022 on the left has arrived from Thurso. When the train from Wick has come to a stand, 26022 will shunt its stock onto the adjacent platform. 26018 will then reverse onto it to form the last train of the day to Inverness. There were three trains a day in this era; there's four these days, at the time of writing, but you'll have to ride on a modern diesel multiple unit. Where's the fun in that?

26037 and 26041 at Georgemas Junction, 13 April 1979. Let's look at the detail. A buffet car, second from the locos, sheer luxury, although the food wasn't that great in those days and was often the subject of media derision! It didn't matter to us, we were grateful travellers. The wisps of steam emanating from the coaching stock heralded a welcome snooze on the journey south. The signal box was the furthest north remaining on the BR system. The wonderful semaphore signals. A 'moment in time'. It felt like it would last forever...

Above left: A Study of Georgemas Junction signal box, 6 September 1976. Just look at those finials! Magnificent. Recently repainted and the old story on the railways goes – 'If they repaint something, it's going to close'! Sure enough...

Above right: Forsinard signal box on a chilly day. A lonely outpost that had at least three passenger trains a day in each direction during the period we're looking at, plus the odd freight or engineering service.

Forsinard station on a sunny day. Tidy and pretty in its simplicity. The old Scottish blue sign an absolute gem. The reason it's so well looked after is down to a mixture of pride from the local railway personnel and the paucity of population in this area to make a mess!

Above left: 26015 and 26035 near County March Summit, 30 November 1981. Double-heading on this line was usually to facilitate swapping the loco kept at Thurso or to make sure the train got to its destination in more extreme weather conditions. The noise from the locos going up this incline was a pleasure akin to a guitar solo at a rock concert!

Above right: Vying with my friend Howard Heyl to get a shot of 26018 at Helmsdale, 6 September 1976. Some interesting vacuum braked wagons in the siding, already looking like candidates for a museum.

26029 arriving at Helmsdale, 2 May 1978. The Post Office minivan on the platform says a lot about the population and its needs in this area! The fitting of small snow ploughs on the buffer beams of the locomotive says even more about the local climate!

26029 at Helmsdale, looking small amid the sweep of the Highland hills. The coaching stock is notable, a 'BCK' behind the loco, meaning a composite vehicle with a small guard's brake compartment, two first and two second class compartments, followed by a buffet car. A perfect combination, particularly if they had someone to staff the buffet car! In the latter days of this service, the northbound buffet was manned as far as Brora, where it closed and the staff member got off to open the facility on the southbound service. A portent of things to come.

Sign of the times; it wasn't just diesel locos that were an endangered species in Scotland during the 1970s! While seeking refreshment in between trains, we often came upon gems like this. 2 May 1978 in Helmsdale. Most of the items in this image will probably end up on one of the multitude of antiques programs that we see on TV these days!

Our driver takes a photograph at Brora, 6 September 1976. I don't know the gentleman, but I'd like to see his photo collection! Due to the many single line sections in Scotland, waiting for the train going in the other direction became a common occurrence and a photo opportunity.

The scene at Brora on 23 April 1981. A wonderful, busy image with human interest and a motley collection of wagons and engineer's vehicles, not to mention the bus! The gent looking after the mail bags seems very relaxed and I'm guessing from the disparity in luggage between the two women that one has come to see the other off on her journey! 26032 on the left awaits 26039 to clear the single line.

The gent on the left looks like the driver that was taking a photo at the same location, back in 1976. Brora, c. 1980. He obviously loves his job!

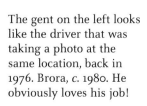

Above: Some of the stalwart diesel chasers (known as 'bashers', in the parlance) actually went to Scotland on family holidays. My old friend, known as 'westernbasher' on Flickr, was one of them. He took this lineside shot of 26041 at Dalchalm, near Brora, on 21 June 1977. The shortest night of the year and very short indeed at that latitude! (Photo by Steve Jackson)

Left: The plaque at Golspie; I doubt that many tourists or railway enthusiasts notice this. I see from recent images on the internet that the bridge has been rebuilt, but the plaque remains. It says: 'This stone is placed here by the united subscription of all who were employed on the works of THE DUKE OF SUTHERLAND'S RAILWAY to record their sense of his patriotic munificence and zeal in promoting the industry and progress of the NORTH OF SCOTLAND and in testimony of their respectful affection 1871.' I wonder if that subscription was voluntary. There's no plaque here to record his family's part in the Highland Clearances in the early part of the nineteenth century...

Study of 26018 at Lairg. A handsome little loco, the Birmingham Carriage and Wagon Works locos served Scotland well until they were required to do more than they were designed for, which, I'm obliged to state, is my personal opinion as an ex-BR driver and that of some retired drivers in Scotland of my acquaintance!

The Victorian cast-iron overbridge, so typical of the railway system and taken for granted by many travellers. This one at Lairg has a builder's plate proclaiming it to be the product of the Rose Street Foundry in Inverness. The year is partially blocked by the superstructure but I'm surmising from the records of Rose Street Foundry that it probably dates from 1875, which means that when this was taken on 6 September 1976 it had passed its 100th birthday!

A rare photo; the only time I saw a Class 24 this far north. Invergordon wasn't a usual passing point for trains between the single line sections. When I took this photo in 1976, a year before I joined the railways, I already knew from experience that the single line token had to pass through the equipment in the signal box before the train could proceed and our train was unloading mail bags, which gave us time to take a couple of photographs.

It looks like a model railway with as much detail within as small an area as possible, but in reality, its 26023 arriving at Dingwall on 8 April 1980. We took this three-coach train to Achnasheen on the Kyle of Lochalsh line. There also seems to be a shortage of white paint in this area; elsewhere in the country the platform edges have an overall white edge, Dingwall is sporting the 'dotted line' motif here! There's too much detail in this image to comment on here!

26041 arriving at Dingwall, 24 April 1981. Fellow railwayman Bernie McDonough takes his shot from the footbridge. When the Woodhead Route closed, Bernie relocated from Dewsnap Sidings TOPS (Total Operations Processing System) office in Manchester to Inverness where he and his colleagues were very helpful in the ensuing years via the internal railway telephone network, which often took the element of chance out of our Scottish roving!

Study of 26015 at Dingwall, 22 September 1980. The footbridge makes a bold frame to the photograph while the man in the boiler suit (not sure if he's station staff!) completes the image. 135 mm telephoto lens gives some 'depth' to the image. The loco number on 26015 seems higher than its fellow class members, I've no idea why!

Thurso had its own status as a 'depot' in those days; it probably still does. A single Type 2 would stay up there all week and, in later days, a Class 37, just to do the 6.75-mile section to and from Georgemas Junction, with the odd variation, timetable experiment and engineer's train. When the loco-hauled trains disappeared from this region, I couldn't ignore the connection that now existed between me and the far north. I once caught 'The Orkney Bus' from Inverness, rather than ride a diesel multiple unit. It wasn't much better so I went against my principles and returned many times by road to get the ferry from Scrabster to Orkney, seeking further glee on the old ferries in that region. As Stephen Dowle, in his book *Class 52 Westerns, The Twilight Years*, makes clear, a pattern was emerging whereby one found something that really takes your interest, only to find that it was doomed to history and subsequently made heroic efforts to capture the final days. We weren't alone.

Caithness, the most sparsely populated county in the UK. On an overcast day, or perhaps because of an overcast day, it can take a grip on the unwary traveller. In the 1970s and 1980s, a window from which you could lean out of the train and smell the heather was part of the journey, a pleasure denied to the modern passenger of air conditioned diesel units. The climb north out of Helmsdale towards County March Summit cannot be appreciated from a seated position, particularly an aisle seat – only the driver of a modern train can enjoy this spectacular view. The construction of the railway to the far north was a literal 'long and winding road'. All of the major projects of railway building in the Victorian era involved political and human struggle and the route to the far north was no exception. Today's travellers cannot appreciate this as we diesel following nomads did on Mark 1 coaching stock in the 1970s, leaning out of the window to take in the atmosphere and the landscape, sometimes in sub-zero temperatures! It was a hard-won railway and we appreciated the effort! It's my all-time favourite county. It's not just a remote outpost, it's a unique part of the UK; the only true wilderness this country has to offer. Its history, from a geological viewpoint, has little to do with the rest of the UK, and from a political overview has more links to Scandinavia. From an open train window, it was pure magic.

Let's look at the names and their relevance in the railways of the 1970s: Georgemas Junction, the furthest north signal box in the 1970s; Scotscalder, great name; Altnabreac, one of the most remote stations in the UK, only accessible by rail (request stop) or forest track; Forsinard, the station in the middle of nowhere – if they ever thought of making a film called *Carry On Up The Railways*, they couldn't have invented this name; Kinbrace; Kildonan; and, a personal favourite, Helmsdale – another Norse name – a station where the line comes down from the Strath of Kildonan to meet the sea and usually a few seals and seabirds before reaching Brora, a council estate in the Highlands. From the railway, that's how Brora looked. Only by road can the older parts of Brora be fully appreciated. Many of these places were where we bailed out and took photographs or changed directions, sometimes taking time to appreciate the local ambience, although maybe that should read 'go for a pint'! In later years, when I utilised a car, these places took on a new significance that I wouldn't have appreciated without my experiences on the railway.

South of Brora, with the exception of Dingwall, the dedicated rail rover would only alight to take a quick photograph. This was a relatively easy manoeuvre due to the time afforded by the mail bags that were being offloaded or uploaded, which didn't take too long in the sparsely populated far north! Continuing south we find Dunrobin Castle where the line from Inverness terminated for some years and only served as a private station for the castle. Further on we find more wonderful names as we head south: Golspie; Rogart; Lairg (a good walk to where Lairg actually is!); Invershin; Culrain; Ardgay; Tain (particularly famous distillery here); Fearn; and Invergordon – once the place of a famous naval mutiny, these days more famous as a rest and repair location for exploratory oil rigs! The last stop before Dingwall is Alness. Before continuing south, let's travel north-east from Kyle of Lochalsh.

Kyle of Lochalsh, 17 July 1975. We'd arrived by sea on the MV (Motor Vessel) *Loch Arkaig* from Mallaig. It wasn't until a couple of years later that we realised how rare this loco was for our journey east. After 1977, in my tenure as a freight guard at Guide Bridge, I worked with a couple of these locos; the combined mileage of those trips was less than the run to Inverness with this machine! Taken from the road bridge over the station.

26044 at Kyle of Lochalsh, 15 August 1977. Most folk that arrived at Kyle of Lochalsh headed for the ferry to Skye. Some went to the pub. My old friend Steve managed to get a rare shot of a light engine movement. Most of us tried to get the Isle of Skye in the background of our photographs and neglected to take this angle! The signal box and semaphore signals are priceless. (Photo by Steve Jackson)

24113 takes us to Inverness, 17 July 1975. Somewhere near Duirnish or Plockton. My first journey out of Kyle of Lochalsh and we'd caught a ferry to get there! It was all new territory to me and the more I saw, the more I wanted to see!

This reminds me of the time when pubs were shut in the afternoon, a legacy of the First World War that lasted until the 1980s, and it meant that we had time to kill! The loco had been shut down for some time, the crew were elsewhere and the weather was gloomy! We spent some time experimenting with a tripod and various angles. I took this view that looks like an old vinyl LP cover; the dreadful flared trousers gives the time period away! Bernie McDonough on the left, me on the track and Hugh Searle on the right next to his 'Class 40 Roadshow' headboard! A 'selfie' long before the users of current technology invented the term! 26029 at Kyle of Lochalsh, 5 May 1978.

Sometimes on a rail rover it was efficient to use other means of transport. On certain days of the week you could ride to Mallaig on the first train from Glasgow, catch the ferry to Armadale, ride the connecting bus service to Kyleakin for the ferry to Kyle of Lochalsh and catch the last train to Inverness, two lengthy dead-end lines in one day. This is an Isle of Skye bus at Kyleakin waiting to return to Armadale after we alighted from it! The Skye Bridge has made this scene a mere memory.

Sunnier weather at Achnasheen, but a sad occasion for me. I had a two week 'Freedom of Scotland' ticket. The first week was spent blissfully chasing diesels with friends, the second week was with the girlfriend, unsuccessfully attempting to mix my enthusiasm with tourism and, in this case, failing miserably! 26029 and 25235 approach from Kyle of Lochalsh on 9 May 1978. The only time I saw a Class 25 on this line! I'd have swapped trains in an instant had I not been committed to visiting Skye... We should have parted company then instead of the following year!

Oddly, there was no snow in the rest of Scotland that week! This is a personal favourite among all the railway photographs I've taken in the far north of Scotland. The location is particularly special to geologists, but that's a story for fans of glacial moraine (great name for a rock band!) rather than a railway narrative! A closer forensic look gives more information. The snow on the tracks tells us that this is the first train since the snowfall. The snow on the back of the semaphore signal tells us that it was an Easterly wind during the snowfall! I've been reading too much Conan Doyle...

Let's deal with the subject of taking a photo out of a window on a moving train before the health and safety police break my door down! I was a railwayman from 1977 to 1995, and all of my railway friends were safety conscious. In these parts of Scotland, in this era, hanging out of a window was obligatory! How else could we record journeys like this? There were few overbridges and no passing trains to watch out for! I'm only sorry that passengers today can't smell the diesel fumes or experience the loss of feeling in your ears and nose at times like this! 26039 near Achanalt, heading west – 24 April 1981.

26046 on a very dark night at Garve – 30 November 1981. Garve wasn't a usual passing point on the Kyle line. I can't recall why we were held here but I couldn't resist trying to get a photograph while we waited for the single line to clear! Using the footbridge as a 'tripod', this was the shaky result in the dim station lights.

The overview – west of Dingwall, we find the equally magnificent, though geologically very different to the far north, Kyle of Lochalsh line. Its fortunes have varied greatly over the years. An early target for Beeching, as was the Far North line, it managed to survive. There was a close call in the early 1970s until the oil industry needed a sheltered facility near Kyle of Lochalsh, after which tourism ensured the future of the line. That's a severe truncation of history but it's sufficient for this look at a specific era! Travelling north-east from Kyle...

Kyle of Lochalsh still retained an atmosphere of its earlier status in the 1960s and early 1970s. Prior to the building of the Skye Bridge, it was the main, but not only, way of reaching the popular Isle of Skye. We happy few diesel 'bashers' found ourselves with time to kill in a place like nowhere else that we'd experienced on our other travels. The ferry was a must. Limited time before the return train meant little exploration of Skye, though Howard and I once hired bicycles just to explore the immediate area! Back in Kyle of Lochalsh, the beer was keg, fizzy, cold and awful, but there was no choice other than abstinence, so we gave in and had some anyway! The station signs evoked an earlier age. Michael Palin was presented with a large station sign from here on one of his first TV travel ramblings, a seemingly momentous railway journey to the British television viewer! A walk in the park to a seasoned rail rover. The overnight train to Fort William and Mallaig gave you the option of a ferry to Armadale on Skye with a bus connection to Kyleakin for the ferry to Kyle and the Inverness train – a very efficient way of doing both lines in one day. The best way to do it was in the summer months. It was the first way I did the journey, catching the twice a week direct boat from Mallaig to Kyle; more than efficient, it was a very pleasant way to spend the afternoon in sheltered waters and superb scenery!

The first time I left Kyle of Lochalsh by rail, after arriving by sea on the motor vessel *Loch Arkaig* from Mallaig, 17 July 1975, was a very special day in my last year as a teenager.

Once again, the weather was nothing to write home about, but we didn't care; we were innocents abroad and absorbing everything Scotland had to offer!

As we left the Kyle of Lochalsh by train, yet more wonderful names drifted past the window: Duirinish; Plockton; Duncraig; Stromeferry; Attadale; Strathcarron; Achnashellach; and Achnasheen, where we crossed paths with the train from Inverness – this was mainly a photo opportunity but a couple of times in later years, when the train from Inverness was running late, there was enough time for a quick drink in the nearby hotel. From Achnasheen, only three stations remained until reaching the relative 'metropolis' of Dingwall – Achanalt, Lochluichart and Garve. All these names seemed mystical to me back then – they still do – and they made me want to return.

The railway lines from the far north and Kyle of Lochalsh came together at Dingwall, a place of many fond memories. The dedicated 'diesel basher' in the far north would encounter this station several times in one day, as it covered both the Far North line and the Kyle line and enabled a seasoned traveller to get the greatest variation of Class 26 locos in one day – a variety unobtainable elsewhere in Scotland. I have to say I preferred to do an entire line in a day but sometimes one's companions were after quantity before quality! Whichever way it went, there were always compensations! The afternoon and evening runs that centred on Dingwall would entail a pleasant sojourn in the station bar with its strange 'trap-shoot' game – a large wall-mounted affair where you obtained a handheld device from behind the bar and took it in turns to 'shoot' the wildfowl that crossed the wall mount (I won't call it a screen, it was a series of flashing lights!) The morning run involved a quick dash to a superb baker's shop for a travelling breakfast to be consumed on the next train.

Inverness. What a great town. The gateway to the far north. A fascinating location. Many rail rovers used it as a base to stay in bed and breakfast establishments. Those among us with a desire to keep moving used the town for a late night drink and a haggis or fish supper before seeking a compartment on the southbound overnight train to Glasgow or Edinburgh. As previously mentioned, seeking a night's bed and breakfast accommodation meant that a huge part of the roving adventure would never be part of the experience. While I felt sorry for those that sought more homely comforts, I envied their facilities. The overnight trains were occasionally crowded but mostly they provided a comfy compartment in a Mark 1 corridor coach with the steam heat lulling you into the arms of Morpheus. All this on top of the beers and supper in Inverness, it was sometimes very difficult to stay awake and enjoy the struggle of machine (or machines, if you had a pair of 26s!) against the gradient up to Slochd Summit, the second highest point on the Highland main line. We did our best but I have to admit to being sound asleep on a few of these journeys! We'd done more than a few overnight journeys on other regions – the Westerns out of Paddington, Class 73s out of Waterloo, the 'Roarers' (81s to 85s) out of Euston, and the Deltics and Class 40s out of Kings Cross – but the atmosphere of an overnight departure out of Inverness had a dreamlike quality that was hard to beat. It wasn't down to the beer, either! On occasion, we would seek the permission of the shed foreman to take some night photographs. They were always accommodating; 'Let us know when you're done, lads.' Scottish hospitality, famed all over the world! Catching the 23.45 to either Glasgow or Edinburgh, and anticipating some sleep after a late night ramble around the shed, was an experience that will stay with me to my dying day.

Inverness. 6 August 1974. After a gruelling overnight journey from Kings Cross to Aberdeen, followed by further snoozing on a Swindon-built diesel multiple unit, I find myself in Inverness for the first time in my life! Wandering around unhindered by authority and generally welcomed, I take my first photos of the area, unfortunately using appalling quality slide film (I won't say the name, but it rhymes with 'naff'), recording the event nonetheless. The star of this image is the footbridge, probably made a few hundred yards from here at the Rose Street Foundry. The gradual dismantling of this bridge can be seen on some following photographs.

The view from a footbridge that no longer exists. My first overview of Inverness station, taken when I was only just eligible to vote! 6 August 1974, a poor month for weather compared to the following years. We were absolute beginners in the 'diesel chasing' world in 1974: we let that train in the foreground leave for Kyle of Lochalsh with the rare 24121 in charge and joined the train behind it for the journey to Georgemas Junction, not realising we could have took 24121 as far as Dingwall... Early days in learning the art of timetables. At least I got a photograph! There's a Royal Mail TPO (travelling post office) on the right to add to the historic vehicles in this image.

Above left: Inverness Shed, or Motive Power Depot, whichever you prefer, way back in the overcast August of 1974 and my first visit. We found the foreman's office and gained permission to walk around, after seeing half the stuff around the shed anyway! They were very accommodating. The back of Rose Street signal box is visible and the contrast between the arched stone portals of the original building and the more modern steel lintels of the brick structure stand out, though when I took this as an eighteen-year-old, I had no idea about such distinctions!

Above right: 26044 on Inverness Shed, late evening, 2 May 1978. Four years later from the previous shot and we were still welcomed by the majority of railway staff, particularly when we mentioned that we were fellow railwaymen! What stands out to me here is the partially filled in archway on the left! In 1978 I took this picture of a loco and thirty-nine years later I'm looking at an architectural alteration in the background! The long winter months just fly past!

26020 ready to leave Inverness for Kyle of Lochalsh, 6 September 1976. The wonderful footbridge is in the first stages of dismantling. We took this train to Dingwall for the Wick train forward; we'd learnt our lesson after missing a ride with 24121 in 1974! I still knock myself out over that mistake!

26041 brings empty coaching stock into Inverness, 15 April 1981. The cast-iron footbridge has now disappeared. This manoeuvre involved some 'propelling' of the coaching stock before it could approach the platform – a practise that's frowned upon in this 'health and safety' age but something we took for granted when I was a guard at Guide Bridge and later as a driver at Manchester Victoria.

The ubiquitous Class 08 shunter, this example seen at Inverness shed in August 1974. A stalwart of British Railways, based on an LMS (London, Midland and Scottish) railway design and many are still extant to this day and not just in Great Britain. They are a testament to the enduring manufacturing quality of the esteemed English Electric company, late of the Vulcan Works in Newton-Le-Willows. I've seen their products as far afield as New Zealand!

Carefully does it! I noticed at an early stage that the platforms in the far north seemed to be a tad lower than the rest of the country. The driver of 27107 and 27007, on an Inverness to Aberdeen service, 22 April 1981, makes an ungainly exit! 'Always back out of a loco cab, unless it's on fire!' Advice I was given by an old-hand driver!

26037 and 26025, on the left, wait to leave Inverness with the overnight service to London Euston. They'll take it (and us) as far as Mossend Yard where an electric loco (83012) will take the train forward. 27012 is on the right with the last train of the day to Aberdeen. The slightly higher angle than usual provided by climbing on a parcels trolley! 22 April 1981.

View from the long-gone footbridge of Inverness shed and Rose Street signal box. The position of the box and the track layout are more striking with the aid of a 135 mm telephoto lens. A superb breakdown crane and its associated wagons is behind the loco; I hope it's found a home on one of the many preserved railways.

40077 and an unidentified Class 24 at Inverness fuelling point, 6 August 1974. Always the gloomiest part of any depot, notwithstanding the weather! Rain or shine, it was always difficult to walk around this part of any depot.

While we're looking at Inverness, any Scottish rail rover worth their salt would be familiar with the Phoenix Bar, a favourite place for a sleeping draught before the overnight journey south. I took this in 1975 with the aid of a mini tripod, a self-timer and a relatively empty pub. The haze is a mixture of negative deterioration and cigarette smoke, note the Claymore sword above the bar and a portrait of the 'Bonny Prince'. The sleep on the ensuing journey south would only be disturbed by a ticket inspection or some severe pyrotechnics from the diesel exhaust on the assault up to Slochd Summit.

'Selfies' have been taken for years with the aid of tripods and self-timers on cameras, and are possibly, for the most part, a little bit more dignified in the 1970s and 1980s. I use the word 'dignified' with tongue firmly in cheek! This was a special occasion: I'm about to leave Inverness with my last steam heat Class 26 for haulage; that is to say, we could only count a loco if we rode behind it! With the aid of some paper towels from the adjacent coach, I marked the event with some cleaning graffiti! That just left the seven freight only members of the class. While we're here, let's say farewell to some things in this photograph – Rose Street Foundry chimney, Mark 1 coaching stock, 26032, my hair, the flares, the wide lapels and 1981!

Inverness to Aberdeen. A route that may lack the glamour of the far north, the rugged beauty afforded by the West Highlands, or the journey from Inverness to Perth, it was still a route that held its own attractions to the roving enthusiast. In the mid-1970s it was the realm of some Swindon-built Diesel Multiple Units (DMUs). These 'bouncy' units had a mini buffet on one vehicle where a cup of 'Maxpax' tea or coffee was an oddly welcome part of the journey. The brew was pretty awful to be honest but when you've been on the go for a few days of continuous travel, it was, to quote an old saying, 'wet and warm'! The units were always warm and provided an extra couple of hours' shuteye in a week of fractured sleep patterns! Consequently, I have few photographs of anything on this line as its main purpose to the rail rover was to get from one city to another and have a snooze along the way.

By the 1980s, the line was pretty much ruled by Class 27s. These trains were also warm from the steam heat provided by the loco and were still a good way of getting an extra few hours of sleep! OK. I'll admit it. I pretty much used this line for catching up on extra snoozing! I apologise to the railway history buffs among you but that's just how it was in those days! I did manage a few photos here and there. Historically, this railway was an important part of the fishing and distillery industries until Beeching and the decline of the fishing industry reduced it to the simple connection between two cities that remains to this day. The distilleries and a couple of other bits are still there, but like many other parts of the railway network, it's a shadow of its former self. Road transport carries most of the whisky these days. As for the fishing industry, well, that's another story...

Inverurie, 6 August 1974. Now you may laugh, and please free to do so, but after a long overnight journey to Aberdeen and a very warm DMU ride from the 'Granite City', something in my teenage brain said 'Get a photo, wake up, you may never be here again!' Poorly composed and taken in a daze, after forty-seven years it becomes a snapshot of railway working that you'll only see again on a preserved railway. Loading stuff on or off a guard's compartment, provincial railway station architecture, the guard's uniform modelled on Gerry Anderson's Captain Scarlet, I miss it all...

An unusual event. The train on the right departed Inverness behind 27107 and failed near the bridge that carries the A9 over the railway. 27003 soon came to our rescue and propelled (pushed) the train to Nairn where we see it 'running round' the train to take it forward to Aberdeen. 15 April 1981.

The scene at Elgin on 20 April 1981. A lovely semaphore signal; the small one allows access to Elgin East Goods, or so it says in one of my railway atlases! 27108 waits for 27007. We had intended going to Aberdeen with 27108 but our 'contacts' in Inverness control informed us of an unusual relief train to Glasgow, so we headed back west behind 27007.

Bernie Mcdonough keeps the door ajar for me as I take a quick shot of 27002 heading our train from Aberdeen to Inverness at Keith. We went straight back to Aberdeen with the same loco for 55016 to Edinburgh – it was basically a 'fill in' move before taking one of the last workings for a Deltic out of Aberdeen. 1 December 1981.

Safe 'window hanging' shot. The adjacent line runs in the same direction and it's clear. Having said that, I was losing the feeling in my extremities to get this photograph of 27002 on 1 December 1981 at Keith.

Waiting for the single line at Insch with 27021, 22 April 1981. By '81, we were more than familiar with this scenario. On this occasion we were headed for Aberdeen, a quick pint, and then back to Inverness with the same loco before our overnight journey south. We'd begun the transition from trying to obtain haulage behind as many different locos as possible to accruing mileage behind specific locos!

This is one of my favourite photographs! Leaving Aberdeen, bound for Inverness after my first visit to the city, we'd arrived on the overnight from Kings Cross and had a bleary-eyed visit to Ferryhill diesel depot before heading west. This was the view from the window as we left. As a lifelong sci-fi fan, it appealed to my visions of a post-apocalyptic world but in reality was the redundant side of the station a year before it was demolished! Taken on 6 August 1974.

Above left: 27021 with leaking steam, about to depart Aberdeen for Inverness. The days of the Swindon built DMUs on this line are long gone and the days of the Class 27s numbered. Some of us stalwarts still made an effort to get some final mileage behind 27s in this region. I was about to 'Photoshop' this image when I realised that the white spots were snow! The weather explains why Julie, my first wife, is running up the platform to take her photograph!

Above right: 26034 ready to leave Aberdeen for Inverness, 24 April 1981. A rare event as Class 27s dominated this line in that era. Another oddity is the colour light signal next to the semaphore signal. Though not yet activated, it's the beginning of the end for a long period of railway history.

40047 at Aberdeen on the mail train to London Euston on 1 December 1981. The train might not be that interesting in 1981, but it attracted the interest of Ronnie Biggs and his fellow felons in 1963, though Biggs' only real role in the robbery was to provide a disgruntled driver that only knew how to drive diesel shunters! 40126 (D326) was the fateful loco on this train in 1963. I worked with it several times in my days as a freight guard.

My history with 40047 as a railwayman at Guide Bridge involved it catching fire, a week out of a works overhaul! They should have let the paint dry before letting it loose on the main line!

The Highland line; rail gradients negotiating mountains – wonderful. Like much of Scotland, hanging out of a window to appreciate it wasn't an option. It was compulsory unless it was an overnight train when serious consideration was given over to some much needed sleep! On occasion we were denied a favoured type of traction on an overnight journey and made a heroic effort to bail out of a train in the middle of the night at somewhere like Aviemore or Kingussie to take our chances in the opposite direction. On one desperate occasion we found ourselves at Pitlochry in the wee hours because we had to head home but couldn't resist a last run for the week with a Class 40 heading north. A surreal experience, looking back at it, but it often paid dividends, including a cab ride in a Class 40 one fateful night. The cab ride wasn't a new experience, having joined the railways in 1977 as a freight guard, but it did help us stay awake!

Other aspects during the day held a fascination. The pass of Druimauchdar, the highest point on the UK railways and the place of many different spellings. I've used the spelling in the 1984 railway atlas but the one on the actual sign doesn't seem to have the letter 'I' on it! The diesel noise out of Inverness up to Sclochd Summit was awesome. The long views among the mountains were spellbinding. The gas lamps at Dunkeld Station. What can I say, this rover ticket certainly gave value for money!

After a quick trip to Elgin on 20 April 1981, armed with information from Inverness Control, we returned to Inverness to catch a relief train for Glasgow that consisted of eight coaches and a single Class 26! Here's that train behind 26044 about to conquer Slochd Summit, 1,315 feet above sea level. A mighty battle of machine against the odds, I had my head out of the window most of the way up the incline and I'm glad I was there to experience it! The noise was awesome.

40164 arriving at Aviemore, 1 October 1980. We were catching this train to Edinburgh so I had to make a dash over the footbridge after taking the shot! My friend, Mr Heyl, was way ahead of me!

Station scene at Kingussie, April, 1980. While waiting for our northbound service to Inverness, one of our number makes some new friends! I suspect these dogs belonged to the signalman as they were hovering around the signal box when not befriending the general public! Bernie wouldn't normally part company with food...

26037 and 26025 cruise past Druimuachdar Summit, 25 April 1981. The highest point on the UK rail network at 1,484 feet above sea level, as proudly proclaimed by that blue sign on the left! No trouble for a pair of these machines in good fettle and good weather. One hell of a struggle for any traction when the weather was unfriendly.

26014 and 26013 en route to Glasgow from Inverness, crossing the splendid bridge over the River Tay at Dalguise. Bridges and viaducts certainly get more ornate the further south one travelled. 10 May 1978.

Above left: 18 April 1981 and we find a station lamp still lit by gas. Not unique, even in that era – a signal box in Manchester, at Denton Junction, was gas lit even after electric track circuit systems were installed! What's unusual here is that it was lit in daylight! It's a shame the glass is cracked; I suspect the cause to be occasional sub-zero weather conditions versus the heat from the burning gas rather than vandalism.

Above right: 26044 and 26037 arriving at Dunkeld, 18 April 1981. The solitary face, hanging out of the window, is my old mate, Bernie McDonough – my 'mole' inside Inverness Control! His colleagues were equally forthcoming with information on the BR internal telephone system when they realised that we were friends of Bernie! I should also apologise to Julie, valiantly carrying all the bags while I take the photographs. If only bags had wheels on them in those days!

26044 and 26037 arrived at Dunkeld. I'm guessing the car belongs to the signalman! The lattice metalwork of the signal post is typical of Scotland. By this time, in 1981, we opted to spend days travelling behind a pair of 26s on their diagram workings with a few side moves to chase any other locos, which were mainly Class 40s and Deltics.

Perth; the heart of Scotland and its ancient capital. From a railway enthusiast's point of view, a place that afforded a great variety of trains. If the locos around here didn't suit you, it's only just over 20 miles to Dundee and the options between Aberdeen and Edinburgh. The station is constructed around a junction and a network of sidings. Here's a view from the interior of the station looking west at 26034. The moped on the platform makes the photograph for me! 2 October 1980.

The early hours of 11 September 1976 at Perth. We'd boarded this overnight train from Edinburgh at Haymarket and would normally have taken this rare pair of 24113 and 26027 all the way to Inverness. We valiantly stayed awake, taking photos like this during the lengthy station stop, eventually turning back to Glasgow at Pitlochry. We'd befriended an Eastfield guard on a trip to Oban the previous day and were determined to return to Oban and spend his last day on the railway with him! A life changing decision; the following days were influential in my joining the railways in 1977!

Above left: One and a half weeks into a two week all line rover, my eighteen-year-old self was in somewhat of a dream-like state, but glad to be back in Scotland. To be honest, it's a miracle I managed to get some pictures! The 'autopilot' worked here enough to capture 24129, 24027 and 40157 at Perth. One of the 24s is having its water tank topped up. Northbound overnight trains would often top up the water tank here to make sure they could maintain the steam heating to Inverness. 14 August 1974.

Above right: 08725 trundles through Perth station with a collection of cars on Motorail flats in June 1980. Many of these cars are considered 'classics' these days, some are not! The proud headboard, 'Perth Station Pilot', is an unofficial title but a nice statement of local pride.

The 'Freedom of Scotland' rover had few restrictions and riding on Motorail services was one of them. Here's one of my second favourite class of locos (Class 52s were always first!) on a Motorail service for London at Perth. It seemed annoying at the time but it turned up later on another train; they usually did! 31 May 1980.

47711 arriving at Perth, 15 April 1981. The Class 47s that became 47/7s were intended to replace the Class 27s on the push/pull Glasgow to Edinburgh services but often turned up on other trains. Note the 'trap points' next to the loco, designed to derail any train that might accidentally pass the signal on the left when showing a red aspect, thus protecting the Glasgow to Aberdeen line.

40173 on a tank train at Perth, 16 April 1981. The nature of rail roving meant that photos of freight trains were relatively rare. We didn't realise that at the time and just carried on regardless, taking photographs of whatever came our way!

This is a working that 'diesel chasers', or 'bashers' as they were more commonly called, were attracted to. An ex-works loco would come out of Glasgow works for a test run, reeking of fresh paint and attached to the train loco in case of failure! Here we see 26019 and 27005 at Perth, 3 April 1980. 26019 is the ex-works machine.

SC51788 at Perth, 8 September 1975. Swindon-built Class 120 DMU on the middle road between the Dundee platforms. Two rare things – these units were mainly used between Inverness and Aberdeen at the time and seeing any train on this piece of track was unusual.

The classic three-quarter view of a train on a station. There's so much more going on here. The classic cast-iron footbridge, the BR vehicle on the platform and the farewell from mother and child to Dad (or Granddad, who can tell?). 40148 at Perth, 2 October 1980.

40148 under Perth footbridge. A different point of view. A plethora of cast-iron hides a phone box that doesn't conform to the national red box that we we're all familiar with in this era! You don't see those cast-iron framed benches these days, apart from preserved railways and a few gardens!

Aberdeen to Perth, another kettle of fish altogether. Type 2 locos, mainly Class 25 and 27s, could be found on the Aberdeen commuter services and further south, the Dundee to Glasgow or Edinburgh 'stoppers', but the majority of the trains were a mixture of Class 40s and 47s, often Longsight-based steam heat Class 40s that the Scottish region 'acquired' from the London Midland for a few days, much to the chagrin of a Manchester-based traveller looking for a rare engine! It has to be said that a certain amount of pride often overcame the disappointment! This coastal route was also more populated than the other lines in the north and afforded some variety in the constant hunt for sustenance.

Meanwhile, back in Aberdeen... Having already looked at the Inverness to Aberdeen line, we're now looking toward the south and east of the city. 55016 is on an evening service to Edinburgh on 1 December 1981. During the last few weeks of operation for this esteemed diesel class, it was a privilege to ride out of the 'Granite City' behind *Gordon Highlander.*

The 17.15 commuter train waits to leave Aberdeen with 25065, 3 April 1980. A fine collection of semaphore signals and a smart looking Class 25, combined with Mark 2 coaching stock. Perfect. When the Mark 2 stock was no longer required by British Railways, much of it found an extended life in Eire and New Zealand, albeit on different track gauges.

Barclay built diesel shunter 06006 stands at Aberdeen, Ferryhill depot, 18 July 1975. A smart looking machine, still carrying a builder's plate and smelling of fresh paint. Many builder's plates mysteriously disappeared in the late 1970s and early 1980s. You might find them on e-Bay these days...

An unusual photograph. The passengers wander along quite unconcerned while the station staff seem very interested! 55014 *The Duke of Wellington's Regiment* is trying to heat Aberdeen Station all on its own! 17 April 1981.

55014 *The Duke of Wellington's Regiment* seems to have sorted out its excessive steam output and stands ready to leave Aberdeen on the 12.40 for Edinburgh. Their halcyon days behind them, the Deltics soldiered on in the same way as their A4 steam locomotive forebears, on less glamorous duties than they were designed for.

As so often happened, the Scottish Region control would purloin London Midland Region Class 40s that had steam heat capability to bolster their passenger services! While slightly annoying to diesel chasers from south of the border, there was an element of pride involved! 40013, belonging to Longsight depot in Manchester, my home town, is about to depart Stonehaven with a Glasgow to Aberdeen train, 23 September 1980.

While waiting for our Southbound train at Stonehaven, 40003 came storming through en route to Aberdeen with a parcels train on the 15 April 1981. Another Class 40 far from home that the Scottish Region had 'borrowed'!

Above left: Stonehaven signal box in the snow. First wife and avid Deltic fan Julie doesn't look very comfortable here, though a steam heated train behind 40061 would soon relieve our discomfort. The signalman seemed quite happy in his cosy signal box! 10 January 1981.

Above right: I came to appreciate Class 47s more when I was trained to drive them in 1990 but here, on 15 April 1981, they either got in the way of the diesels we were after or provided a means to an end! In this case, I needed 47220 for haulage and it got us here to Stonehaven to catch a Deltic.

55008 *The Green Howards* on an Aberdeen to Edinburgh service arriving at Stonehaven, 15 April 1981. A magic period along this line when almost anything could turn up from a High Speed Train, which hadn't achieved a high speed since south of Newcastle, to a humble Class 25!

On preserved railways these days, this is a much coveted window view. Back on 17 April 1981, near Stonehaven en route from Dundee to Aberdeen, it was just me on one side and Bernie on the other. My first wife was having a read and patiently waiting for Deltic 55014 on the next train south. 40061, an actual Scottish-based loco doing what it did best and sporting a splendid paint job, still carrying its works plates. The plates mysteriously started to disappear around this era. You can still see them on preserved locos, in museums and on e-Bay!

40161 coming into Stonehaven, 25 September 1980; an easily identifiable machine due to the paint damage on the front. Compare with the photograph of it on a Motorail service at Perth back in May of the same year. Notice the lattice type signal post that had been replaced by April the following year when I photographed 47220 next to it.

40158 steaming away quietly and waiting for the guard's signal to leave Arbroath en route to Aberdeen. There is an interesting selection of architecture here, which overshadows the signal box. A fine selection of ground signals and a trespass warning that I suspect carries a more significant fine these days. 2 October 1980.

47272 arriving at Arbroath, 4 May 1978. There's some interesting things in this image: the 'loading gauge' hanging off the wall behind the station sign; the proprietors of the Station Hotel purveying Drybroughs Ales and the ladder that's precariously placed under the hotel sign.

The real star of this photo is the station sign 'Dundee Tay Bridge', with its helpful directions for accommodation. 40161, on 18 July 1975, plays a secondary role. Much in this image has been consigned to history.

27038 on Dundee shed, July 1975, with the usual mulch of diesel oil underfoot from years of leakage. This is the only photo I have of this loco and I only have two photos taken on this long gone shed!

55008 *The Green Howards* gets some attention from some young enthusiasts at Dundee, 15 April 1981. A modern form of 'brass rubbing' to obtain a paper souvenir. I'd bet serious money that these lads, all these years later, still have that memento, rolled up, tucked away in a corner of the house, hidden away from the wife and kids only to see the light of day when old mates visit!

An immaculate 26019 coupled to 27005 in the bay platform at Dundee, 3 April 1980. Recently out shopped from overhaul at Glasgow works and on a test run, the diagrammed loco (27005) remains with the train as an insurance policy against failure!

Invergowrie, between Dundee and Perth. I only alighted at this station twice in my Scottish wanderings. Whether it was due to a late running train to avoid missing a connection or merely a way to get a different photograph, the reason is lost in the mists of time! 25044 arriving on 25 September 1980.

Things to come. 37027 on Dundee, 31 May 1980 – an early invader in the realm of the Class 26s and 27s. The nature of pre-privatisation British Rail meant that locos like these, built in the mid-1960s, when supplanted by other machines 'down south', would replace older machines in the north. This is sometimes called the 'cascade' system and is further evidence of the north/south divide.

Taken on my camera by Julie, my body language says it all. We'd just alighted from a Deltic-hauled train at Dundee to go to Perth in search of Class 40s. At the time, 15 April 1981, we tried to avoid non loco-hauled trains and a single car DMU seemed like a low point. These days, a 'bubble car', as they were known, and 55000 in particular, would be considered a rare event to be enjoyed for the 20.25 miles to Perth! Times change.

I could have corrected the horizon with modern technology but I'm leaving the image as I saw it through the viewfinder. A dramatic view of 26044 leaving Invergowrie, heading for Dundee with a nice display of 'clag'! Steam enthusiasts prefer the exhaust of a coal fired loco, but I'll take the risks of diesel output against soot in my eyes any day! I know that's not very PC these days; it's all about one's age, experience and preferences!

40162 arriving at Invergowrie, 16 April 1981. The second and last time I visited this station, on this occasion, it was for no other reason than photography! If 'proper' trains still called here, I'd go back!

An unusual view of a Glasgow to Dundee service at Perth in April 1980, with 27014 at the front. The guard of the train is struggling to close the doors against something he's just loaded while the banner repeater signal above and to the left of him tells me that the signal in front of the loco is still showing a red aspect, so there's no rush! All this and the station clock! A moment in time!

59

Dundee to Edinburgh. This route has the two most iconic railway features on the Scottish network – the bridges over the Tay and the Forth. The journey over the River Tay after Dundee affords a view of a grim reminder of the Tay Bridge disaster of December 1879, as the original stone piers are still extant on the Eastern side of the current bridge. When travelling over the superb Forth Bridge, it's worth bearing in mind that the designer of the ill-fated Tay Bridge, Sir Thomas Bouch, had a proposal for a bridge over the Forth. It was a lot cheaper than the eventual design but, for some reason, they opted for something a tad sturdier.

North of the Forth there are a few variations aside from the mainlines that held an attraction for those more interested in trainspotting than travelling, most of which come together at Inverkeithing. From a rail roving perspective, they were lines that might be experienced on a Sunday diversion or a ride on a suburban service, but they were otherwise a mystery. The depot at Dunfermline Townhill was the only unwelcoming place I ever encountered in Scotland.

The arrival into Edinburgh held the delight of a run past the legendary Haymarket shed – a golden name in the history of the railways, particularly the crack expresses between Edinburgh and Kings Cross in the halcyon days of steam, right up to the last days of the formidable Deltics. This was followed by a brief stop at the incredibly dismal (in the 1970s and early 1980s) Haymarket station. There were reasonable places near to Haymarket where one could avail oneself of the local hostelries and food after the walk back from the shed, followed by a choice of traction for the last 1.25 miles into Edinburgh Waverley, but the station itself was a depressing place in those days.

Another example of a safe 'window hanging' photo. From Dundee to the covered part of the Tay Bridge had no obstructions on the left-hand side, plus if you wrapped the camera strap around the wrist and guessed the angle, you didn't need to lean out bodily! The piers of the old bridge provide an eerie reminder of the Tay Bridge disaster of 28 December 1879.

40101 heading south, 2 October 1980.

Inverkeithing, a place in Scotland that we didn't frequent much – usually only on Edinburgh suburban services that were loco hauled. On this occasion we spent enough time here to see this train twice! 20205 on a ballast train, 24 September 1980.

20205 has obviously run around its train (the wagons are still loaded) since the previous photograph and is now headed south! Bonnet-first views of Class 20s were rare south of the border, so we always made an effort to photograph them in Scotland.

The classic view of the iconic Forth Bridge from Queensferry. A Class 47 heads north on some air conditioned stock, probably for Aberdeen. This coaching stock hastened the end of classic diesels in Scotland, which lacked the capability to operate the air conditioning and electric train heating.

Not quite the classic view. A 135 mm telephoto shot with my trusty Yashica FR1. 26044 trundles along the Forth Bridge with a local service from Edinburgh to Dundee, meaning it stops virtually everywhere!

Definitely not a classic view of the Forth Bridge! The time honoured technique of wrapping the camera strap around my wrist, checking the bridge is clear and guessing the angle. I could have corrected that with modern technology but I chose to leave it as taken, a reminder of days when this was possible. The traveller of today cannot experience the olfactory pleasures that accompanied this view; the salt water smell of the estuary, the ferrous odour of all the metalwork mingling with the fumes from the locos, all possible from an open window. 26021 and 26014 en route to Inverness, 30 September 1980.

Haymarket shed, famous for its association with the crack services between Edinburgh and London Kings Cross and a great attraction in the 1970s and 1980s for its varied collection of diesels. 47524 and H. T. Heyl, taken from inside the shed, July 1975. Four character headcodes were still in use in this era.

26031 and 26010 on Haymarket shed, July 1975. Spot the difference. 26031 is an Inverness allocated machine and still shows the bodyside gap at the front where single line token catching equipment used to be stowed, also the mini snow ploughs could be useful in the weather of the far north. 26010 is a Haymarket machine and has none of these features; it seems to have a builder's plate still in place under the number.

Above left: I think Howard is picking up his camera case off the somewhat tatty platform at Haymarket while 26028 heads for Edinburgh, 5 April 1980, on an ex-Dundee train. Haymarket station in this era had a very rundown atmosphere but that made it all the more attractive to us as we were transported to a time that we were too young to have experienced!

Above right: Sunday engineering trains at Princes Street Gardens, Edinburgh. The travelling public dread events like this, but to us rail rovers, it was an opportunity. Apart from the photos, there were the diversions that took us over freight only lines or past difficult to reach geographic locations like Millerhill depot. Since I took this, some lines around Edinburgh have been reinstated to passenger use, which says a lot about the current scene in Scotland.

47543 on the right, passing 26002, 40054 in the background – 12 September 1976.

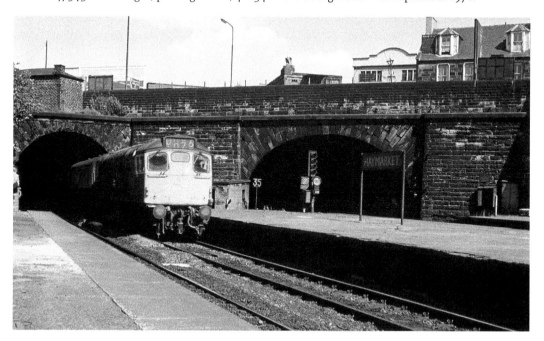

Edinburgh to Glasgow push/pull service arrives at Haymarket, July 1975. We took these services for granted on our Scottish Rovers to the point that we took very few photographs of them. The cost of slide film was a huge consideration at the time. If only digital photography had come along forty years earlier!

What makes this photograph for me is the train crew on the right; one of them is lost in conversation, and the other is watching me! The rest of the image is another moment in time: the 16-ton coal wagons and the loco are long gone, and Haymarket Station has been 'updated'. Time marches on...

Heading for home after a week on the rails of Scotland we opt for an overnight train out of the capital and are rewarded with 40077, at least as far as Carstairs. I set up the tripod and let the camera (Yashica FR1) decide the exposure. The tower of the North British Hotel on the top left and the steam drifting behind the loco make a fond memory for me.

Deltics and Edinburgh, strawberries and cream, Laurel and Hardy, Neil Armstrong and Buzz Aldrin, Morecambe and Wise. The list goes on; one without the other is inconceivable! 55013 *The Black Watch* stands at Edinburgh, 31 August 1981, arrived from Kings Cross.

Above left: After a short respite at Haymarket, 55013 prepares to return to London from Edinburgh, 27 August 1981. Scant months to go before the end of Deltic operations, *Black Watch* acquitted itself well. I hoped that it would make it into the preservation scene, but it wasn't to be. Considering there were only twenty-two of them, it's amazing that six of the class made it into preservation, seven if you count the prototype!

Above right: 55017 *The Durham Light Infantry* arrived at Edinburgh. I'm not sure about the exact date but I can tell you that it's 1981 and it is August or September when I arrived with it on four journeys – three from Kings Cross and one from Newcastle! It's towards the end for the Deltics and they're relegated to the rarely used platforms, out of the way of the newcomer HSTs (High Speed Trains).

I was never enamoured by the overall 'blueness' of Ektachrome film but I think it works quite well in this image of 47524 arriving at Edinburgh, July 1975, We avoided these locos like the plague in those days but I came to a better appreciation when I worked with them. The fact that some are still around in 2017 from their origins in the mid-1960s speaks volumes.

Now, we're talking! Scotland's own Type 2s in the capital on an extensive diagram between Inverness, Glasgow and Edinburgh. 26037 and 26044 wait to leave Edinburgh, 18 April 1981. We only took them to Perth, because we knew the Saturday night diversions south of Carlisle were going to produce a Class 40 over the Settle line. Having done that, we returned to Scotland post haste!

The hours before catching the overnight train at Edinburgh were usually spent in The Guildford Arms before a walk across the valley to a shop near the Royal Mile that did an excellent baked potato with haggis. Despite that, I seem to have been *compos mentis* enough to get a tripod shot of 26025 and 26037 with the overnight for Inverness, 24 April 1981.

Deltic 55007 *Pinza* is dwarfed by the architecture of Edinburgh, in this case, the Art Gallery. It's artfully putting on a fine display of fumes and thanks to the medium of photography, taking its own place in history!

My contacts on the internet inform me that the gentleman in the photo is loco inspector Jimmy 'Tam' Farrell – the spelling varies but the respect is manifest. He was a friend to enthusiasts and railwaymen alike and is, sadly, no longer with us. I was taking a photo of the loco and accidentally got a shot of a true railwayman. Edinburgh, 7 September 1976.

South and west of Edinburgh. In the era we're looking at, it was basically a choice between North Berwick and Berwick-on-Tweed on the rover ticket. Overnight trains during engineering works might involve some variation, but these lines weren't traversed on rover tickets, they were a by-product of the latter days chasing Deltic operations when travelling on free passes. Some of these lines have reopened to passenger traffic since those days, which says a lot about Scotland's commitment to rail travel. Millerhill depot on the south-east side of Edinburgh was a particularly difficult place to visit and was only usually seen from the window of a diverted train during engineering works!

North Berwick, the only time I ever went there! I suspect Howard's influence as a 'line basher' had something to do with it! The Ektachrome 'blue' dates it to July 1975; regardless of my notebooks, I didn't use this film again! It wasn't that bad, it was just too blue. Railway photography seemed better served by Kodachrome. Other slide films were available... Does anyone still use slide film? I've still got two rolls of unexposed Kodachrome 64!

Above left: Berwick-upon-Tweed. Technically not Scotland, but like Carlisle, it was a destination available on a Scottish Rover. Here's a 'selfie' from my mini tripod that turned out to have an historic significance. Mr Heyl and myself (I'm the one on the left!) pose at Berwick-on-Tweed as 55009 *Alycidon* leaves for Kings Cross on 7 September 1976. Fast-forward to 9 May 2014; thanks to an old mate from Guide Bridge that was retiring from the railways, Martin Pennington, we spent a day with him and this machine, driving it up and down the East Lancashire Railway! Funny old world...

Above right: Remember when pubs shut in the afternoon? No? Then you're not as old as me! Time to kill in between trains at Berwick, set up the tripod and do a double exposure, turning my jacket inside out for one of them – this was the result! Probably inspired by Monty Python...

Isn't it cute? 03066 at Berwick-upon-Tweed. Based at Newcastle, the journey from there to here must have been somewhat gruelling on this! I've travelled some distance on the footplate of many diesel shunters and they're memories I'd rather forget.

40198 in what I believe was called the 'Fish Dock' at Berwick-upon-Tweed. I thought it an unusual place to leave a main line loco until I found out that there was a depot here, which, like my first depot on the railways, Guide Bridge, was a 'signing on point' with no allocated engines. Effectively a stabling point.

03079 in the Fish Dock at Berwick. It's noticeable that most photographs of Class 03s usually have a flat wagon next to the loco. This was to provide some extra brake force when engaged in 'loose' shunting operations – a practice that I suspect is now consigned to history, since I left the railways in 1995. I'd be surprised if that Ford Capri on the platform is still around!

Taken from the Fish Dock at Berwick-upon-Tweed, 55008 *The Green Howards* makes an impressive plume from one of its two stroke diesel engines as it departs for London Kings Cross on 19 April 1981.

Dundee and Perth to Glasgow; serious territory for the serious diesel basher! Famous names like Gleneagles and Stirling, much greater density of population and therefore more trains. The all stations services could turn out almost anything and the long distance trains often produced a beloved Class 40! One particular morning train from Glasgow to Dundee often featured a loco fresh out of Glasgow Works, gleaming as though it had just been built rather than emerging from a major overhaul. Reeking of fresh paint that probably wasn't dry, virtually rebuilt and raring to go, these machines weren't trusted to go out on their own! Not only was this service double-headed to ensure that it made it to Dundee, it also carried a lot of extra personnel – mainly loco inspectors and diesel fitters. These were particular entertaining trains to catch. There was always an air of mystery about them. Would we make it to Dundee without incident? Usually! It did provide an opportunity to photograph a pristine diesel and that was certainly rare!

Howard on the left in his trademark cap, watching proceedings at Perth, that's our team on this particular occasion. It seems we're joined by a younger contingent, the next generation of enthusiasts. Apart from the diesels we shared the common bond of living on the railways and out of a bag for a week! 26023 on a Dundee to Glasgow service, 7 April 1980.

26037 and 26025 pause at Perth en route from Inverness to Glasgow, a train we caught throughout on 25 April 1981. This became the preferred traction if a Class 40 wasn't available, so much so that we did over a thousand miles in four days with this pair!

Every picture tells a story. The obvious one is the arrival of 26025 and 26037 at Stirling. Less obvious is my old friend PK, leaning out of the first coach! A Metropolitan Cammell DMU rests in the north bay platform. The painted tyres as plant holders are a common motif in this region. The briefcase is mine, usually containing my camera and two or three lenses, the Scottish Region timetable and a couple of cans! 25 April 1981!

16 April 1981, a busy day for loco haulage. My diary shows seventeen separate entries for that day, although three of those were for one overnight train! 40162 turned up on three occasions. We've alighted here at Stirling off the 0640 ex-Glasgow and fought our way through the steam to take a photograph! A rare sight to see the train heating boiler safety valve venting to atmosphere and let's not forget the tyres on the platform!

An afternoon scene at Stirling, 22 September 1980. 40063 seems to have lost a few cables, judging by the conspicuous holes in the buffer beam! Though a stalwart Scottish Class 40, it often turned up in the north-west of England. I rode behind it on an advertised excursion out of Buxton in Derbyshire!

Stirling fuelling point, 6 April 1980. It was unusual to see a Class 40 in this siding; it caught fire the previous day and was dumped here until it could be dragged somewhere for remedial work. Note the damaged bodyside paintwork. It must have been moved here in a hurry because they've blocked in a DMU and left the loco foul of the adjacent siding!

A loco that seemed to follow me around! I worked with it several times when I was a freight guard at Guide Bridge. I go on holiday to Scotland and it turns up to keep me company again! 40091 at Stirling, 2 October 1980.

Scottish Region seemed quite happy to employ single Class 20s on minor duties, in railway parlance, 'trip freights'. An obvious disadvantage in one direction is the reduced visibility for the driver, though they managed well enough in the age of steam with a single cab! Elsewhere on the system, these machines were more often seen in pairs. 20207 is seen here at Bishopbriggs on 5 November 1979.

Glasgow Queen Street station, my favourite station in Scotland. It might not have the sprawling nature of Edinburgh Waverley or the vast spread of Glasgow Central but that's why it's so special. In the 1970s and 1980s it dealt with the huge number of trains coming through the two-track tunnel to a dead end station with a consummate ease. The station itself resides under a single canopy roof, reminiscent of Liverpool Lime Street and equally as graceful. Food and drink was within easy reach and the staff were friendly. By the time I took this image of 26037 and 26033 on 27 September 1980, we'd taken to carrying an enamelled brew can with us, using the staff mess rooms to make some coffee and, hopefully, some contacts! It often worked!

27025 makes some fumes as she (locomotives are always 'she', trains are 'he' – an important distinction that many film makers fail to observe!) departs from Glasgow Queen Street in April 1980.

Above left: 27204 heads a Glasgow to Edinburgh push/pull service in 1976 at Glasgow Queen Street. These diesels that served so well on other lines in Scotland were literally flogged to death on the Glasgow/Edinburgh services that required constant high speed running on an intensive timetable. It was a great service for a while, but it was a disservice to these locos, well beyond their design parameters. I enjoyed many rides on the push/pulls but remember saying to my old friend Howard that 'they can't keep this up'. It seems I was right.

Above right: A poignant photograph of 40072 at Glasgow Queen Street, poignant in that I'd arrived there behind a different loco, set up the tripod and camera to get a few shots, and hoped the Class 40 would turn out later. If it did, I missed it. I never got to ride behind this loco, one of the sixteen (of 200) that eluded me. 7 September 1976.

40165 at Glasgow Queen Street, 3 October 1980, very early in the morning. We'd arrived at Queen Street from Carlisle via Mossend and Eastfield to find this beauty on the blocks and, this time knowing the loco diagrams, did a quick move to Stirling and back for breakfast before returning to Glasgow for a ride behind this machine! The atmosphere at Glasgow Queen Street in the wee hours was magical to me in those days. We rode behind it from here to Stonehaven after the brief excursion to Stirling.

One of my favourite loco 'portraits', probably due to the magnificent wall that forms the backdrop to this view of 25228, the station pilot at Glasgow Queen Street. August 1981.

Julie and I had been in Scotland for nearly two weeks, breaking the rail roving with a visit to friends in Carluke and a quick stay on the Isle of Arran. On 4 October 1980, we were ready to go home and arrived in Glasgow Queen Street with that in mind, only to find 40061 at the head of the next Aberdeen service. Of the 200 Class 40s built, I missed sixteen of them to ride behind. On this date there were only three extant locos left that I needed for 'haulage' and 40061 was one of them! We could only take it as far as Stirling, but that was enough for me. Julie, posing with the loco, was always happy to travel the rails but would have preferred a Deltic on the front! 40061 turned up again in the future but I wasn't to know that at the time; so many were being withdrawn I had to get a ride behind it when the chance arose!

37026 on Glasgow Queen Street, 31 July 1980. Early days for this class on the West Highland line and the beginning of the end for the BRCW locos that dominated this area for many years.

Another arrival in Scotland that meant the end for the Class 26s and 27s were the Class 47/7s, specially fitted to work the Glasgow to Edinburgh push/pull services. 47711, later to be named *Greyfriars Bobby* at the suggestion of Scottish newspaper readers, stands at Glasgow Queen Street.

A mini tripod gives this view a dramatic angle but the driver walking towards us with a determined stride really completes the picture! 40168 on Glasgow Queen Street, 17 April 1981.

Early trips to Glasgow weren't complete without a visit to Eastfield depot. Using the directions in the invaluable *Loco Shed Directory*, an Ian Allen volume that no self-respecting enthusiast would leave home without, you'd end up here at Springburn station for the walk to the depot. 20048 and a brake van are seen here with a motley collection of units on 2 February 1976. I'm not saying the area was a bit 'rough' in those days but the off licences were like banks – you made your purchases through security screens!

A rare shot for me, the 'standard' three-quarter view, or is it? 27113, one of the adapted locos for the Glasgow/Edinburgh push/pull services stands at Eastfield, Glasgow, 6 December 1974. 27113 was not its original number and not its final number! Confusing? It made life difficult for train spotters! It also had an unreliable handbrake; note the wooden wheel chock under the first bogie. All the Class 40s carried them for the same reason!

Above left: I love this image, though it's a bit sad as it's a line of scrapped locos waiting for the cutter's torch at Eastfield depot. 06001 and 24006 in the foreground, 12 September 1976. I think it's a good example of the atmosphere that a black and white photograph can convey, which is difficult to reproduce in colour.

Above right: Roaming around Eastfield depot. A friendly place to railway enthusiasts in the 1970s before the days of high visibility jackets, hard hats and steel toe capped boots! It's a wonder we managed to survive. The 'Health and Safety' police were a few years away; their main protagonists were probably not born when I took this on 12 September 1976!

The signalman's view of Eastfield depot from Cowlairs box. The last day of our three-day association with Jimmy Morgan, a top man. Saying farewell to his friend the signalman, and taking us along with him to record the event, he was a shining example of Scottish hospitality.

Another gloomy day and a sad sight. D8616 in Glasgow Works awaits the cutting torch. I was too young to have known these locos in service but thanks to Derby Research Department keeping a couple of them going, I did, at least, see one on my home territory in Manchester. The Diesel Traction Group rescued one from industrial use and I finally got a ride behind it on the Severn Valley in 2015.

The 'Freedom of Scotland' ticket – or indeed any rail rover ticket that encompassed Scotland – included a few ships and this one was very special: the *Maid of the Loch*, a paddle steamer on Loch Lomond. I had three memorable journeys on this vessel as a break from chasing trains. It's had a chequered history and has languished for some years at Balloch Pier; hopefully it will cruise the loch again someday.

The West Highland lines. Oban and Mallaig; the part of Scotland that tourists and railway enthusiasts frequent the most, so I'll not dwell on too much detail here. I preferred the far north but that's a personal view. There's no denying the scenic splendour of the West Highlands, particularly Rannoch Moor, but I always felt more 'at home' in Caithness! The station names in the west have more of a Gaelic origin compared to the far north, reflecting the historic borders between the Norsemen (Vikings) and the Gaels. There are notable historic sites on this side of Scotland; the concrete viaduct at Horseshoe Pass is a favourite among photographers so I'll miss that one out this time! The skyline at Oban featuring the McCaig Tower is unavoidable!

27016 and yours truly at Oban, 3 May 1978. Taken on my camera by Hugh Searle, part of the three-man team on this particular Scottish Rover. Sadly, a scan from a photograph as the negative is long lost, but it remains a fond memory for me, nonetheless.

Yet another rare event! 55021 arrived at Oban, 23 August 1981. Not a rail tour, but an advertised excursion train from Edinburgh, complete with Mark 3 air conditioned stock! We were valid to ride on it with our Scottish rover tickets, though we couldn't get a seat! We didn't care! A Deltic to Oban! It was worth standing in the end vestibule! You can tell by the age of the punters filing past the loco that this wasn't an enthusiasts' train, though the teenager in a BR uniform looks a bit suspicious!

55021 *Argyll and Sutherland Highlander*
at Oban, waiting to return to Edinburgh
on an advertised excursion. Standing in
the corridor for the outward and return
journey proved a bit tiring but well
worth the effort! It turned out to be a
good rehearsal for journeys on the West
and East Coast Main Lines in later years!
The chance to ride the West Highland
line with a Deltic was extremely rare.
A feast for English Electric fans here as
two Class 37s share the station with our
train, the magnificent McCaig's Tower
dominating the skyline.

Oban Station, 10 September 1976.
A photo taken 'on the hoof'! A quick
capture on a rapid turnaround! Look
at the station sign, proudly stating
'British Rail'. That was the company
I joined in 1977. It covered the UK, had
the biggest fleet of ferries in Europe,
a road transport infrastructure and an
impressive hotel chain and I was proud
to become a part of it. How the mighty
have fallen...

The guard joins us on the West
Highland line! I don't know who the
kid is but our train guard is Mr Jimmy
Morgan on his last day working for
British Rail before moving to South
Wales to work with his brother. We'd
met him the previous day on the
same working, Oban and back from
Glasgow. We got quite friendly and he
invited us to join him for his farewell
trip; in return he fixed it for us to
have a cab ride. 11 September 1976.
(Photo by H. T. Heyl)

Above left: The aforementioned cab ride on the West Highland line, not long after Connel Ferry, 11 September 1976. 27015 with an EQ vacuum brake system, though we didn't know that then. In subsequent days as a freight guard, I never met a driver that liked it and when I finally got to drive vacuum-braked trains in 1990, the EQ system had vanished and vacuum brakes in general were on the way out. There's still plenty of vacuum-braked trains to this day on the nation's preserved railways.

Above right: The snow has just started to fall as 27032 arrives at Corrour, making the image start to blur. The steam heat boiler is evidently working. The summit board, just to the right of the loco, proclaiming the height above sea level to be 1,350 feet. One day they'll replace that with the equivalent in metres, but it won't have the same feel to it! 10 April 1979 and we're eager to get out of the snow!

Glasgow Queen Street, 11 September 1976. Eastfield guard Jimmy Morgan on the left has just worked his last train before leaving Scotland for a new life off the railways. That twenty-year-old 'hippy' on the right is me. Bags with wheels would have been welcome in those days! At least I developed a strong grip. That guard in the background seems to be struggling with something that modern trains couldn't possibly accommodate. (Photo by H. T. Heyl)

After getting to know Jimmy over the preceding days, we opted to join him for farewell drinks with his railway colleagues in Glasgow and spend the Saturday night sleeping on his furniture, a better option than a risky overnight journey to Carlisle and a possible oversleep! It was an interesting Saturday night in Glasgow, particularly heading for the last bus amidst the hordes of Bay City Roller fans that had tipped out from a home town gig!

Sunday 12 September 1976 dawned and after a welcome bacon buttie, we accompanied Jim to Eastfield depot to hand in his 'traps' (guard's equipment), stopping en route for a visit to Cowlairs signal box and a walk around the shed. Jimmy, in his leather jacket, looks like an extra from the film *Get Carter*. After a lunchtime pint near Eastfield, we shook hands and said farewell. We never saw him again but his hospitality and the mutual respect among his railway colleagues remain an inspiration to this day.

Howard, on the left edge of shot, is looking into a twin lens reflex camera that belonged to me and cost less than £10! 20099, returning from an engineering job, has just been re-manned and is probably on its way to Cadder Yard.

Glasgow to Edinburgh, the beating heart of Scotland's railways. Fewer than 50 miles separates the two cities whether you go via Falkirk High or Falkirk Grahamston but there's a million miles between them in cultural differences. Even the accent and dialect is different, as are those of the far north, just as my Manchester voice differs from the good folk who live 40 miles to the east and west of me. I still find this fascinating. It drew me back to Scotland just as much as the railways – I wanted to experience and study it more. My reluctant days at school and college were fading fast from my faulty memory. The railways and Scotland actually made me want to learn.

In the mid to late 1970s, Glasgow to Edinburgh was the realm of the Class 27s; one at each end with five or six coaches in between the locos. The intensive timetable meant that these machines were thrashed to within an inch of their lives and, in many cases, it severely shortened them. I was a Western Region diesel hydraulic fan and loved my native Class 40s in the North West, but these noisy little critters on this route gave me a new respect for the products of the Birmingham Railway Carriage and Wagon Company. I have to add that after a few days of 24 hours a day travelling, they were also a good train for a quick kip! On one occasion I woke up and couldn't remember which direction we were going! It was extremely disorientating!

South of Glasgow. Tagging along with Howard – who to this day is trying to travel over as many different lines as possible – meant doing a few branch lines. While I was happier travelling behind some noisy machines on the main line, I didn't mind exploring some of the byways of the railways, including the original Glasgow Underground system before it was replaced by the new 'Clockwork Orange' upgrade.

27025 at Glasgow Central, 4 June 1982. Unlike most of the Scottish Region, bar the far north, Class 27s weren't common here in the 1980s, only seen on these trains that brought passengers from the Dumfries and Galloway region, having started its journey at Carlisle, and the odd Sunday diversion.

I don't have to consult my diaries to tell you that this is a Sunday! The black and white photo makes it the 1970s and the fact that it's a push/pull service from Glasgow to Edinburgh at Central station means that engineering work is afoot! I didn't know it at the time, but this was a rare event. 27201 at the front (27211 at the back!) awaits the driver and second man to finish their discussion with the platform staff. The second man's shoes are just visible, unlike the rest of him! 12 September 1976.

After the introduction of electric-hauled services in May 1974, this was the usual scene on this side of Glasgow Central. 87002 *Royal Sovereign* and 85015 – 26 August 1981. 87002 is the only Class 87 still working in the UK at the time of writing. Twenty-one members of the class went to Bulgaria, the rest were scrapped!

This is probably one of the rarest photographs I ever took! 85040 at Wemyss Bay! It was on an advertised excursion from Manchester to Rothesay on 19 March 1977. This loco worked it from Preston. Many of my internet correspondents claim this event to be almost unheard of, diesels being the norm on special trains in this era.

85018 at Weymss Bay, 19 March 1977. Not only did we have the privilege of arriving here behind 85040, they sent another of the class to shunt the stock for the return journey! It was years later when I found out what a momentous occasion this was as all excursion trains on this branch were traditionally diesel-hauled.

Scottish roving on a freight train! A day off from passenger trains finds me accompanying my old friend and ex Guide Bridge man Graeme. He's the driver of 25035 on trip 25, a local working out of Motherwell, 23 June 1980. As soon as that Class 87 has cleared the junction we can proceed to Lanark.

A real rarity, the Lanark branch with a locomotive. Motherwell depot trip freight behind 25035 is signal checked, giving me a photo opportunity! I was a freight guard in Manchester at the time and was able to render some assistance, making the day go a bit quicker for all concerned.

Carluke station from 25035, 23 June 1980. At the time it was the home station of the driver, my great friend Graeme. Both of us left the railways a long time ago for other shores...

Taken from 25035, heading south from Mossend; another Class 25 passes us on another 'trip' working. 23 June 1980.

Stranraer, 8 September 1976. A long gone scene – the ferry terminal has been relocated. 25025 has been 'recycled', though we used to call it 'scrapped' in those days! The *Antrim Princess* was a historic ship – the first 'drive through' ferry – ending its days, as so many other ships, in the Mediterranean.

After a long overnight journey that involved a change of trains in the early hours at Carlisle, which was always difficult, we managed to get to Stranraer. Not a lot to do if you weren't catching the ferry so we took some photographs. The light of dawn and the station frames 25025 on the right, 8 September 1976.

25025 to the rescue! The DMU that should have took us back north had failed with flat batteries. 25025 was pressed into service off its intended freight working; lucky for us, though it was a cold journey without train heating!

Swindon-built DMU with flat batteries arrived at Ayr behind 25025. We really should have taken this to Glasgow but the gent in the picture that's running, my old friend Howard, had other ideas, which meant spending the afternoon on the Clyde on the TS *Queen Mary II*. I'm grateful for his vision. It was a splendid day of cruising, which many Scottish rail rovers never availed themselves of. The Clyde and Loch Lomond were part of the rover ticket and we certainly took advantage of it.

25002 on Ayr shed, 8 September 1976. A quick trip around the depot before spending the day on the Clyde. The early built Class 25s were common in this part of Scotland.

27204, displaced from its former glory on the Glasgow/Edinburgh high speed services, is seen here at Dumfries on a Glasgow to Carlisle train. 1 June 1982.

Carlisle, like Berwick-upon-Tweed, is not a part of Scotland, but it was always part of the Scottish rail roving experience. Here's a portrait of 26037 at Carlisle, a long way from its usual territory.

The one that got away! That lady on the right was; and still is, a Deltic fan. On this occasion, two days after we were married, we attempted to catch the APT (Advanced Passenger Train) out of Glasgow. It came into the platform and was subsequently declared a failure. We made the best of it and did some other travelling within Scotland. 370 002 is the errant example of the class about to be taken to the 'naughty steps' at Shields Road Depot, 8 December 1980.

The one that didn't get away! Finally caught up with an APT but it turned out to be a disappointing run. Point to point was impressive but it didn't fit in with the scheduled trains and seemed to spend more time at station stops than it did on the move! All that money spent in bizarre technology to make the train tilt when they only had to ask a motorcyclist about leaning into a curve. The Italians were way ahead of this simple matter of physics, which is why our current 'tilting' trains, the Pendolinos, originate there.

We ended up at some scary places. One of Howard's branch line ventures was quite memorable. It was south-west of Glasgow; I'm not going to specify the location, but I have to say it was a different time and a more nervous era. We found ourselves with some time to kill and located a bar near the station. As we entered the establishment it was obvious this was no ordinary bar. There were boxes piled up all over the place and, as it was my round, I approached the bar. 'Two pints of heavy, please.' The barman leaned across the bar and put his finger on my neck, taking it down through my open shirt to see if I was wearing a crucifix. Satisfied that we weren't of the Catholic persuasion, he served us with some beer. Hopefully we live in more enlightened days in this century.

Ayr to Stranraer. Another line less travelled. That's not to say that we weren't interested in this journey, it was just awkward to do it with a loco rather than a diesel multiple unit in the 1970s. The bare choice was an overnight journey from Carlisle on the boat train from Euston for a DMU back to civilisation, or not do it! Howard's desire to cover the line won out. I'm glad it did. Not only did I get some of my favourite black and white images of the Stranraer location, but our DMU for the return north had flat batteries and had to be dragged by a Class 25! Sadly, we got off that train at Ayr when we should have taken it all the way. We missed a photo opportunity at Glasgow, opting for a sail around the Clyde on the TS *Queen Mary II*. What were we thinking? We swapped one historical event for another. Our journeys at the time were very much based on good luck than good management!

Motherwell to Carlisle. Getting away from the populated areas and the branch lines of Glasgow, the West Coast Main Line takes on a rugged, scenic nature. Travelling north from Carlisle it gave a taste of things to come for those intrepid souls setting out for a week or more on a nomadic adventure with a 'Freedom of Scotland' ticket in their pocket. Those heading south were either on overnight trains and risking oversleeping past the validity of their ticket, or heading home and looking wistfully at the hills around Beattock, wishing they could stay a bit longer...

A Personal Overview

The early days of cooperation between railways and shipping, a nod to the era of steam railways and steam ships, lingered on in Scotland. The basic business reasoning behind this was to attract those foreign tourists who eschewed the car – whether to avoid driving on the left-hand side of the road or just to be entertained from a train window or the deck of a ship, who knows? The real audience and punters for the rover ticket in the 1970s and 80s were the growing number of diesel enthusiasts – the guys and a few gals who didn't experience the era of steam. The few folk who were of a generation that sought out the last days of some rare diesel locos and the areas that still retained a 'personality' in a world that was rapidly acquiring a depressing corporate blandness.

The aforementioned Mr Heyl had, by this time, initiated me in the dark arts of black and white photography; a day or a week out on the rails was followed by several days in the dark room – the acetic acid smell of the photo chemicals, the drip of the tap cleansing the final images. Happy days, or rather, nights, spent in the dark!

It took us several weeks to develop the shots from a 1975 Scottish Rover and some of the negatives still languish unprinted. Our income didn't match the demands of our enthusiasm in those times. Eventually digital technology will come to our rescue, but not just yet...

Like all the railway regions, Scotland had its own character and locomotives. We can thank the fiasco of the early dieselisation programmes for the variety that still persisted around the country in the 1970s. The details of the early diesel days have been dealt with in many books over the years, so I won't go into them here. I'm personally grateful for the 'fiasco' of British Railway's inter regional managerial dysfunction during the 1950s and early 1960s because it meant that my contemporaries and I were able to gain great pleasure in the variety of diesels that were afforded to the roving traveller. Many of these people, including me, gave up on the BR system in the 1980s and sought further railway pleasure on foreign shores. The golden years of Scottish roving finished forever in the late 1980s.

In the current era, it seems that some diesel locos can still be found in Scotland, but beyond the remaining HSTs, you'd better be prepared for an overnight journey on the sleepers or an uncomfortable squeeze into one of the modern diesel multiple units. In the summer months it's possible to journey between Fort William and Mallaig behind a steam loco on some old coaching stock. It's less than 42 miles and it's an incredibly scenic journey; I might get around to it one day, but it won't be the same without a Class 27 on the front...

It wasn't always diesels that caught my attention in Scotland! 60009 *Union of South Africa* lurks next to the wall at Edinburgh Waverley in April 1981. The current era finds steam alive and well, working many months of the year between Mallaig and Fort William, not to mention the preserved railways of Scotland. I suspect the former is mainly due to the *Harry Potter* films and fair play if it keeps the line and steam going!

Acknowledgements

This a very personal journey. Any opinions are obviously my own. The nature of rail roving meant that the majority of photographs are based around railway stations or sheds, and for that I make no apology – that's how it was.

Thanks to Mam and Dad, without whom I wouldn't be writing this!

Many thanks to all my companions on these travels in Scotland. I was rarely alone, but quite happy when I was! My main thanks go to my lifelong friend, Howard T. Heyl, for starting me out on a journey that I'm still travelling and to our wives for continuing to indulge us!

P. K. Williams (Pickled Kidney on Flickr). A top man, his contribution goes 'beyond rubies', to quote a late mutual friend.

A very special thanks to Margaret, who was reasonably happy to be a 'computer widow', while I assembled this volume.

Inevitably, I checked some stuff on Wikipedia, so I'm prepared for corrections! We'll see, I always hope for the best. Most of the information is from diaries, journals and notebooks, all notoriously unreliable and for that, I apologise. I just hope to entertain.

If anyone wishes to talk to me or add a correction, I can be found here – https://www.flickr.com/photos/deadmans_handle

A final thanks to Radio 4 and the World Service for keeping me company along the way.

Be seeing you,
Arnie Furniss